Protecting the
Dispossessed

A BROOKINGS OCCASIONAL PAPER

Protecting the Dispossessed

A Challenge for the International Community

Francis M. Deng

THE BROOKINGS INSTITUTION
Washington, D.C.

Brookings Occasional Papers

THE BROOKINGS INSTITUTION is a private nonprofit organization devoted to research, education, and publication on important issues of domestic and foreign policy. Its principal purpose is to bring knowledge to bear on the major policy problems facing the American people.

On occasion Brookings staff members produce research papers that warrant immediate circulation as contributions to the public debate. Because of the circumstances of their production, these Occasional Papers are not subjected to all of the formal review procedures established for the Institution's research publications. As in all Brookings publications, the judgments, conclusions, and recommendations presented in the Papers are solely those of the authors and should not be attributed to the trustees, officers, or other staff members of the Institution.

Copyright © 1993
THE BROOKINGS INSTITUTION
1775 Massachusetts Avenue, N.W., Washington, D.C. 20036

Library of Congress Cataloging-in-Publication Data:

Deng. Francis Mading, 1938–
    Protecting the dispossessed : a challenge to the international community /
Francis M. Deng
        p. cm.
    Includes bibliographical references and index.
    ISBN 0-8157-1826-8 — ISBN 0-8157-1825-X (pbk.)
    1. Refugees. 2. Refugees—Government policy. I. Title.
    HV640.D46 1993
    362.87—dc20
                                                    93-5812
                                                      CIP

9 8 7 6 5 4 3 2 1

The paper used in this publication meets the minimum requirements of the American National Standard for Information Sciences—Permanence of Paper for Printed Library Materials, ANSI Z39.48—1984.

Foreword

About 25 million people worldwide are reported to be displaced within their own countries, a number that far exceeds the estimated 18 million refugees. Like refugees, the displaced are victims of civil wars, internal strife, communal violence, forced relocation, and gross violations of human rights; they lack food, shelter, clothing, safety, basic health care, and education. But because the displaced remain inside their countries, they do not receive the same attention, protection, and assistance that the international community gives those who have crossed international borders as refugees.

The plight of the displaced is, however, beginning to draw international concern. In March 1992 the UN Commission on Human Rights requested the secretary-general to appoint the author, Francis M. Deng, as his special representative to study their problems, the international legal standards for their protection and assistance, the mechanisms for enforcing the standards, and any additional measures the United Nations might take to improve their situation. The author visited countries in Africa, Europe, and Latin America and held discussions with governments, opposition groups, nongovernmental organizations, and citizens. This book has been inspired by the author's study submitted to the commission in March 1993. It reviews the state of the law and enforcement mechanisms and the situation in the countries the author visited. It analyzes internal displacement as an aspect of a wider crisis of nation building. Finally, it offers recommendations about what the international community can do to address not only the symptoms represented by displacement but their causes in the domestic conditions.

The author would like to express his appreciation for all those who helped him, in particular the collaborative contribution made by research teams from Harvard and Yale Universities. The Harvard researchers included Henry Steiner, director of the Human Rights Program, his colleagues Deborah Anker and Jennifer M. Greene, and their students Maria Stavropoulou and David Thronson. Abraham Chayes first suggested the idea of collaboration with the Harvard Law School. The researchers from the Yale Law School included Drew Days, director of the Schell Center for Human Rights, and Michael Reisman and their students, Andrea Bjorklund, Carl Goldfarb, Hillary Greene, Gregory Hunt, Eleanor Lacey, Andre LeSage, David Kirk, and Colleen Westbrook.

The author also thanks the Refugee Policy Group, particularly Dennis Gallagher, the executive director, and Roberta Cohen, senior human rights advisor, who worked very closely in preparing the study, and Kate Lawler, who assisted with research and planning.

Working groups organized by the Refugee Policy Group and the Brookings Foreign Policy program met to discuss the concepts of the study and the progress of the work. Those who attended included Liz Barnet, Fred Cole, Janelle Dillard, Charles Dunbar, Tom Farer, Robert Goldman, Leon Gordenker, Michelle Klein-Solomon, Paula Lynch, Susan Forbes Martin, Larry Minear, Kathleen Newland, Diane Orentlicher, Louis B. Sohn, David Stewart, Michel Veuthey, Margaret Willingham, and Roger Winter.

The author's colleagues, Terrence Lyons, Khalid Medani, Donald Rothchild, John Steinbruner, and Susan Woodward made invaluable intellectual contributions. Terrence Lyons assisted with editing the various drafts, and Khalid Medani contributed substantively to the research on and writing of the case studies. Kirsten Soule typed and retyped numerous drafts, and Susanne Lane kept work on schedule. Jim Schneider edited the manuscript, Rebecca Krafft proofread it, Susan Woollen prepared it for typesetting, and Patricia Deminna compiled the index.

The author also benefited from contributions made by the staff members of the Center for Human Rights, UN Office in Geneva, especially Daniel O'Donnell, Georg Mautner-Markhof, and Brigitte LaCroix.

Because of the unique character of the study and the sources used, the manuscript has not been subjected to the formal review and verification procedures established for research publications of the Brookings Institution.

This study was supported by the Carnegie Corporation of New York, the Rockefeller Foundation, and the Rockefeller Brothers Fund.

The views expressed in this book are those of the author and should not be ascribed to the people whose assistance is acknowledged above, to the United Nations, or to the trustees, officers, and other staff members of the Brookings Institution.

BRUCE K. MACLAURY
President

August 1993
Washington, D.C.

Contents

Abbreviations and Acronyms

ANERA	Nationalist Republican Alliance
CIREFCA	International Conference on Refugees in Central America
CPP	Cambodian People's Party
CSSDCA	Conference on Security, Stability, Development, and Cooperation in Africa
FMLN	Farabundo Marti Liberation Front
FUNCINPEC	United Front for an Independent, Neutral, Peaceful and Cooperative Cambodia
ICRC	International Committee of the Red Cross
KPNLF	Khmer People's National Liberation Front
NDA	National Democratic Alliance
NIF	National Islamic Front
OAS	Organization of American States
OAU	Organization of African Unity
ONUSAL	United Nations Observer Mission in El Salvador
PDK	Party of Democratic Kampuchea
SDM	Somali Democratic Movement
SNC	Supreme National Council
SNM	Somali National Movement
SPLA	Sudan People's Liberation Army
SPLM	Sudan People's Liberation Movement
SPM	Somali Patriotic Movement
SSDF	Somali Salvation Democratic Front

SSLM	Southern Sudanese Liberation Movement
UNESCO	UN Educational, Scientific, and Cultural Organization
UNHCR	UN High Commissioner for Refugees
UNICEF	UN Children's Fund
UNOSOM	UN Observer Mission in Somalia
UNTAC	UN Transitional Authority in Cambodia
USC	United Somali Congress

Protecting the Dispossessed

Introduction

Principles of Protection

When President Jimmy Carter first "startled the world with his insistence that the United States would henceforth take seriously its commitment to the advancement of human rights without conventional regard for national boundaries," many around the world and within the United States considered the attitude recklessly idealistic.[1] Some disparaged it as a naive view of foreign policy, which, they reasoned, should serve discernible national interests and not altruistic moral objectives. Others argued against the policy by invoking the relativism of the values behind the principles of human rights. Few today, however, would express such views without some serious pause, whatever their political persuasion or national affiliation.

One only has to take a cursory look at the language of recent UN resolutions on human rights and humanitarian issues to realize that gross human rights violations are being exposed. One category of victims currently drawing international attention is internally displaced persons. Worldwide, the number of people displaced within their own countries far exceeds the number of those who have crossed international borders and become refugees. The most recent estimates set the internally displaced population at 25 million and the refugee population at 18 million.

---

1. Alice Henkin, ed., *Human Dignity: The Internationalization of Human Rights* (Queenstown, Md.: Aspen Institute for Humanistic Studies, 1979), p. v.

1

Despite the intensity and scope of internal displacement, there is no adequate system of protection and assistance for displaced people. Various elements of the International Bill of Rights provide protection on the basis of equality for all humankind, but no specific legal instrument covers the particular needs of the internally displaced, and no specific institution is mandated to address those needs. The United Nations is, however, beginning to recognize this flaw in the international system and is starting to take corrective steps.

This book is a by-product of the increasing international concern with the plight of the internally displaced. On March 5, 1992, the UN Commission on Human Rights adopted resolution 1992/73 (see appendix A) in which it requested the secretary-general to designate a representative to seek from all governments views and information on human rights issues related to internally displaced persons and to examine existing international human rights mechanisms, the applicability of humanitarian and refugee law and standards to the protection of displaced persons, and the provision of relief assistance to them. The secretary-general was also to seek information on these matters from the specialized agencies, relevant UN organs, regional intergovernmental and nongovernmental organizations, and experts in all regions. The secretary-general was to submit a comprehensive study on the subject to the commission at its forty-ninth session in February–March 1993.

As the mandated representative of the secretary-general, I requested information from the sources specified in the resolution, consulted widely with organizations, institutions, groups, and individuals within and beyond the UN system, and visited five countries in Europe, Africa, and Latin America to consult with governments and other pertinent sources. At its forty-ninth session the Commission on Human Rights considered the resulting study, endorsed its findings and recommendations, and decided to renew the mandate of the representative of the secretary-general for two years to continue the work, especially compiling legal instruments, monitoring performance, entering into discussions with governments and other actors, and reporting annually to the commission and the General Assembly. The study submitted to the commission has been thoroughly revised for this book so as to focus attention on the existing legal and institutional principles of protection, the prevailing conditions in the affected countries, and the urgent need for international response to the challenge of internal displacement.

The Challenge

A report prepared by the Secretariat and known as the *Analytical Report of the Secretary-General on Internally Displaced Persons*, submitted to the Commission on Human Rights at its forty-eighth session in 1992, led to the adoption of resolution 1992/73 that mandated the new study. The report found that natural disasters, armed conflict, communal violence, and systematic violations of human rights are among the causes of massive involuntary migrations within state borders. Vulnerable and unable to find places of safety, internally displaced persons often suffer persistent violations of fundamental human rights, and their basic needs go unmet.[2]

From the perspective of the international community, the crisis of the internally displaced is that they fall within the domestic jurisdiction and are therefore not covered by the protection normally accorded refugees. Usually refugees have fled from imminent danger across international borders; internally displaced persons are generally those who have been forced to leave their homes and sources of livelihood but are still within the borders of a country undergoing violent internal conflict. The fundamental rights and human needs of displaced persons are at least as threatened as are those of refugees. Indeed on the whole, the need of the internally displaced for international assistance and protection appears to be greater. Nevertheless, the legal doctrine and institutional arrangements for protecting and assisting the internally displaced are far less developed than those that apply to refugees. International responses to emergencies involving the displaced have in some circumstances been undertaken by the United Nations High Commissioner for Refugees (UNHCR) and, outside the UN system, by the International Committee of the Red Cross (ICRC). But in the absence of clear mandates and an international body with special responsibility for their protection, the international responses have been ad hoc, limited, and unsatisfactory.

An extensive correlation exists between the causes of displacement, their implications in terms of the needs they create, and the responses of the governments concerned. Where the causes are natural disasters, a national consensus to provide protection and assistance is likely, and the

---

2. *Analytical Report of the Secretary-General on Internally Displaced Persons*, E/CN.4/1992/23 (United Nations, 1992), para. 6.

government often assumes responsibility with the assistance of the international community. But by far the most serious cases emanate from armed conflicts in which the displaced become the responsibility of no one because neither side is concerned with them or they become the victims of one or another side. It is particularly in these circumstances that the protection and assistance of the international community are needed, often urgently, although they are frequently difficult to provide because of the jealous defense of sovereignty by governments that are unwilling or unable to provide equal protection to all nationals.

The challenge posed by the problems of the internally displaced must be viewed in the context of events since the end of the cold war. Long-suppressed ethnic and religious conflicts have been unleashed in many parts of the world. But the international community is also more willing than before to address these problems and try to develop mechanisms comparable to those developed for refugees to protect and aid the internally displaced. The challenge, however, is dependent on an even larger context. Resolving the problems of the internally displaced must ultimately mean addressing the causes of displacement, which, in many instances, means making efforts toward resolving conflicts, ensuring peace and security for all, and guaranteeing the rights of citizenship without discrimination, a task that may call for international intervention with all its attendant problems.

Legal Protection

Human rights law and humanitarian law may be considered the principal sources of protection for internally displaced persons. Along with refugee law, they may also provide a basis for articulating further protections. Although these bodies of law are conceptually distinct, they have influenced and informed each other and have also contributed to a corpus of laws that could be applied to the problems experienced by internally displaced persons.[3]

Unlike refugee law, which generally applies only when a border is crossed, or humanitarian law, which applies to situations of armed

3. For example, human rights law is part of the standard interpretive framework for the protection and assistance of refugees. Humanitarian law principles also have contributed to expansions of assistance to refugees.

conflict, human rights law proclaims broad guarantees for the fundamental rights of all human beings. The International Bill of Human Rights, composed of the Universal Declaration of Human Rights, the International Covenant on Civil and Political Rights, and the International Covenant on Economic, Social, and Cultural Rights, represents the corpus of human rights law recognizing the inherent dignity and equality of all human beings and setting a common standard for their rights.[4] These instruments guarantee a panoply of rights applicable to the situations common to the internally displaced, varying from the so-called negative rights—that no one shall be subjected to torture, arbitrary interference with family, home, or privacy and, under article 17 of the Universal Declaration, arbitrary deprivation of property—to affirmative rights, such as the rights to an adequate standard of living and to liberty and security of person.

The International Covenant on Civil and Political Rights and its Optional Protocol elaborate on the principles set forth in the Universal Declaration and provide a procedure for formal complaints and investigations.[5] The International Covenant on Economic, Social, and Cultural Rights is the primary source of obligations to ensure the economic and social well-being of all persons. Among the specific rights that form the basis for assisting the internally displaced are the right to food, clothing, housing, and medical treatment. Other international legal instruments—the Convention against Torture and Other Cruel, Inhuman, or Degrading Treatment or Punishment, the International Convention on the Elimination of All Forms of Racial Discrimination, the Convention on the Rights of the Child, and the International Convention on the Protection of the Rights of All Migrant Workers and Members of Their Families—contain provisions offering a wide range of relevant human rights guarantees. Regional human rights instruments, including the African Charter on Human and Peoples' Rights, the European Convention for the Protection

4. *Universal Declaration of Human Rights*, A/810 (United Nations, December 10, 1948); *International Covenant on Economic, Social, and Cultural Rights*, A/6316 (United Nations, December 16, 1966); and *International Covenant on Civil and Political Rights*, A/6316 (United Nations, December 16, 1966). See Frank Newman and David Weissbrodt, *Selected International Human Rights Instruments* (Cincinnati: Anderson Publishing, 1990), pp. 11–15, 16–24, 25–41.

5. *Optional Protocol to the International Covenant on Civil and Political Rights*, A/6316 (United Nations, December 16, 1966). See Newman and Weissbrodt, *Selected International Human Rights Instruments*, pp. 41–44.

of Human Rights and Fundamental Freedoms, and the American Convention on Human Rights, provide similar and in some cases additional guarantees.[6]

Although human rights law provides a basis for protecting and assisting internally displaced persons, it does not directly address some situations affecting them, such as forcible displacement and lack of access to humanitarian assistance. With respect to humanitarian law, the four Geneva Conventions of 1949 and the Additional Protocols of 1977 reaffirm the principle that in situations of armed conflict those not directly participating in the hostilities shall be treated humanely.[7] Article 3, common to all four Conventions, categorically prohibits violence to life and person, the taking of hostages, and outrages upon personal dignity of persons in situations of "armed conflict not of an international character occurring in the territory of one of the High Contracting Parties."[8] It affirms a due process requirement and imposes a duty to provide the sick and wounded with medical care. The obligation to apply article 3 is absolute for each party to the conflict and is not contingent on reciprocity.

The 1977 Protocol II to the Geneva Conventions is also applicable to internal conflicts that involve "organized armed groups . . . under responsible command" exercising control over territory. The specific need for protection of persons internally displaced by civil conflict is recognized in article 17(1), which states that "the displacement of the civilian population shall not be ordered for reasons related to the conflict unless the security of the civilians involved or imperative military reasons so demand," in which case "all possible measures shall be taken in order

6. *African Charter on Human and Peoples' Rights*, CAB/LEG/67/3 (Addis Ababa: Organization of African Unity, 1982); *European Convention for the Protection of Human Rights and Fundamental Freedoms*, UN Treaty Series (United Nations, 1950); and *American Convention on Human Rights*, OEA/Ser.L/V/II.23, doc. 21 (Washington: Organization of American States, 1975). See Newman and Weissbrodt, *Selected International Human Rights Instruments*, pp. 52–61, 61–88, 97–111.

7. *Protocol Additional to the Geneva Conventions of 12 August 1949, and Relating to the Protection of Victims of International Armed Conflicts*, A/32/144/I.l.M. 1391 (United Nations, 1977) [hereafter Protocol II]; and *Protocol Additional to the Geneva Conventions of 12 August 1949, and Relating to the Protection of Victims of Non-International Armed Conflicts*, A/32/144/I.L.M. 1442 (United Nations, 1977) [hereafter Additional Protocol II]. See David Weissbrodt and Frank Newman, *International Human Rights: Law, Policy, and Process* (Cincinnati: Anderson Publishing, 1990).

8. See, for example, *Geneva Convention Relative to the Protection of Civilian Persons in Time of War*, 75 UN Treaty Series 287 [hereafter *Fourth Geneva Convention*]. See Weissbrodt and Newman, *International Human Rights*, pp. 701–06.

that the civilian population may be received under satisfactory conditions of shelter, hygiene, safety, and nutrition." And according to article
17(2), "civilians shall not be compelled to leave their own territory for
reasons connected with the conflict." Protocol II adds collective punishment, terrorism, rape, enforced prostitution, slavery, pillage, and threats
to commit any of these acts to the list of prohibited actions. The Geneva
Conventions confer special status on the International Committee of the
Red Cross, which is mandated by the Statutes of the International Red
Cross and Red Crescent Movement to protect and assist victims of armed
conflict as provided for under humanitarian law.[9]

Existing international standards specifically concerning the rights of
internally displaced persons under humanitarian law, however, have
limitations. Although article 17 of Protocol II is a useful provision, it
applies only to persons displaced because of armed conflict and only to
states that are party to Additional Protocol II. Moreover, the justification
for displacement based on the need to provide security is broadly construed. The requirement of "responsible command" would make the
armed conflicts in the former Yugoslavia, and certainly Somalia, marginal
cases under the Conventions and the Protocols. Article 17 would also
appear not to cover situations where populations move because of
generalized violence and fear—as opposed to being ordered or otherwise compelled to move—which is often the case with the internally
displaced.

As for the significance of refugee law to internally displaced persons,
one of the most important rights drawn from it may be the right to seek
asylum. Internally displaced persons have much in common with refugees; the critical and in some instances only distinction is that crossing
an international border turns an internally displaced person into a refugee. Although some have argued that this is an arbitrary distinction
limiting the applicability of refugee law to internally displaced persons,
it is of enormous consequence because a displaced person's presence in
a country other than his or her own initiates coverage by a well-established protective mechanism and affords the person rights recognized
under international law. In particular, crossing a border is vital to the
concept of *non refoulement*, the right of refugees not to have to return

9. For a discussion on this see Peter Sandoz, "Fact Finding Mission Established,"
International Committee of the Red Cross Bulletin, no. 195 (April 1992).

to a country that would persecute them—the core of refugee protection.[10] Although "safe havens" have been created in such countries as Iraq and the former Yugoslavia to protect the internally displaced, the existence of such zones does not preclude persons from exercising their rights to leave and seek asylum.

There has been no formal redefinition of the term *refugee* for the purposes of states' obligations under the 1951 Convention and the 1967 Protocol, but the mandate of the UN High Commissioner for Refugees has been extended to include persons displaced in a manner other than that anticipated by the convention.[11] In some cases, UNHCR coverage now extends to those displaced for reasons other than a well-founded fear of persecution on the grounds outlined in the convention and even extends to those who have not crossed national boundaries. Regional instruments such as the Organization of African Unity Convention and the Cartagena Declaration provide variations broadening the definition of *refugee* by considering other causes of dislocation—external aggression, occupation, foreign domination, or events seriously disturbing public order in either all or part of the country of origin or nationality— although the definitions still retain the criterion of crossing a border.[12]

Generally, the protection internally displaced persons can derive from refugee law is limited by the very fact that unlike refugees the people affected are within the borders of their own countries. Any extension of refugee law to them can be only partial and therefore only partially protective.

All in all, legal protection falls short of providing the internally displaced with protection adequate to their specific needs. Displacement is often created by, and in turn results in, crises in which the rights normally taken for granted—physical security, shelter, food, water,

10. Non refoulement has been recognized as customary law for all refugees, even those fleeing generalized violence who do not fit one of the traditional categories of the convention. See Guy Goodwin-Gil, "Non-Refoulement and the New Asylum Seekers," *Virginia Journal of International Law*, vol. 26 (Summer 1986), pp. 897–920.

11. *Convention Relating to the Status of Refugees*, UN Treaty Series 137 (United Nations, April 22, 1954). The convention was opened for signature in 1951.

12. *Organization of African Unity Convention Governing the Specific Aspects of Refugee Problems in Africa* (Addis Ababa: Organization of African Unity, November 22, 1984). The Cartagena Declaration is reproduced in *Annual Report of Inter-American Commission on Human Rights*, OEA/Ser.L/V/II.66, doc. 10 (Washington: Inter-American Commission on Human Rights, 1984).

health care, and other basic amenities—are acutely compromised. Under those conditions, both the norms and their application need to be tailored to the nature and the magnitude of the crisis. In effect, the challenge becomes more than one of implementation and enforcement. Just as certain categories of vulnerable groups such as refugees, the disabled, women, and children, require special regimes for protection, so do the internally displaced.

The *Analytical Report of the Secretary-General on Internally Displaced Persons* concluded that there is at present no clear statement of the human rights of internally displaced persons or those at risk of becoming displaced. The applicable international law is a patchwork of customary standards: parts apply to all persons, parts only to certain subgroups of displaced persons, such as those displaced as a result of armed conflict, and parts may not apply in certain situations, such as an emergency threatening the life of the nation, or may apply only during a state of emergency. Internal displacement constitutes a humanitarian and human rights crisis of major proportions that calls for clear guidelines that could be applied to all internally displaced persons, regardless of the cause of their displacement, the country concerned, or the legal, social, political, or military situation.

Legal scholars have varying judgments on the desirability of seeking further promulgation of rights for the internally displaced. Some argue that if an effort to define rights did not succeed or resulted in a weak document, the protection offered by existing human rights instruments might be compromised. Some even contend that the present condemnation of those who violate the human rights of the internally displaced is based on the presumption that these persons are already protected by law. To argue that there is no adequate protection might be unwittingly to provide a pretext of no violation because there are no clearly defined standards to violate.

On a more empirical ground, however, a case can be made that between the laws providing for normal human rights and those providing humanitarian protections there is a vague area in which the needs of the displaced are marginally covered and not specifically targeted. Ultimately the matter is more important than a theoretical discussion of whether there is adequate protection in the law. The reality is that the internally displaced constitute millions of vulnerable people whose desperate needs are not being adequately met and who have no institution mandated to care for them. What is needed is more than the letter of the law in a document; it is a greater awareness of the problem and practical measures to provide speedy remedies, although a clear statement of pertinent standards would be a significant complement. Conceived as part of a dynamic process of decisionmaking, law becomes not an end but a means to be molded as need requires, both as an educational prescription and a sanction.

For that purpose there is broad support for immediate measures that need not depend on whether existing laws give adequate coverage. These measures should include compiling existing standards and analyzing them to determine their adequacy for protecting the rights of the displaced. This compilation could be restated as a code of conduct with principles that could guide governments, other pertinent actors in a crisis, and all those concerned with the practical means of providing protection and assistance. Compilation, analysis, and restatement of principles could also generate a declaration, which, while not an enforceable legal document, would have a moral and administrative force that would be important in raising consciousness and rallying international public opinion. As a culmination of a concerted effort, and depending on the evaluation of the need, a convention on the rights of the displaced could be prepared and adopted.

Meanwhile, however, the needs of the internally displaced masses demand that minimum standards of existing law be observed and internationally sanctioned. Ideally, justice requires that the standards will apply to all persons falling into the intended category. In reality, achieving such comprehensive application is a utopian goal. Balancing aspirations and practical limitations almost certainly means the criteria for determining that a violation of the standards has occurred will be ambiguous. The choice of actionable cases will also have to be highly selective.

In cases of human rights violations, people whose rights have been violated need legal recourse to courts or other law enforcement mechanisms. But displaced people hardly ever resort to seeking remedies through established legal procedures. The meaningful source of protection and assistance available to them becomes their right of access to humanitarian relief, which means the right of physical access by the international community and the right of the international community to be given that access.

Enforcement Mechanisms

Responsibility for assisting internally displaced persons lies in the first instance with the home country, but if a country is unable or unwilling to meet the minimum standards required by humanitarian or human rights law, the protection of the population involved, including the provision of humanitarian assistance, becomes a matter of international attention. The General Assembly, for example, in resolution 43/131, Humanitarian Assistance to Victims of Natural Disasters and Similar Emergency Situations, recognizes that displaced persons outside the original definition of refugees are within the scope of international, and therefore UN, concern. In resolution 46/182 of December 19, 1991, which created the position of emergency relief coordinator, the General Assembly again affirmed that humanitarian assistance for victims of natural disasters and other emergencies was a matter of international import.[13] The secretary-general has also approved guidelines stressing "the responsibility of States to take care of the victims of emergencies occurring on their territory and the need for access to those requiring humanitarian assistance."[14]

Increased concern with the relief needs of the internally displaced, however, has not been accompanied by increased attention to protection. In the UN human rights system, there is still no mechanism whose mandate explicitly covers the needs of the displaced to be protected. The Commission on Human Rights has special rapporteurs and working groups on enforced or involuntary disappearances, summary or arbitrary executions, torture, arbitrary detention, religious intolerance, the use of mercenaries, and the sale of children. But the overall circumstances of the internally displaced do not fit into these categories, and these people generally remain outside commission consideration. It is therefore widely agreed that a way to focus on displaced persons from within the UN human rights system is urgently needed. Given the commission's special procedures mechanisms, such a focus could be achieved by

---

13. *Humanitarian Assistance to Victims of Natural Disasters and Similar Emergency Situations*, G.A. res. 43/131 (United Nations, 1989); and *Coordination of Humanitarian Assistance*, G.A. res. 46/182 (United Nations, December 19, 1991).

14. Boutros Boutros-Ghali, *An Agenda for Peace: Preventive Diplomacy, Peacemaking and Peace-keeping*, A/47/477; S/24/11 (United Nations, June 17, 1992).

renewing and expanding the role of the representative of the secretary-general or appointing a special rapporteur of the commission or a working group composed of independent experts.[15] The need for an approach that could cut across UN agency jurisdictions persuaded the commission to renew and expand the mandate of the representative of the secretary-general.

Measures taken within the framework of the Commission on Human Rights, although significant, do not adequately address the challenge of providing comprehensive international protection and assistance to the displaced. One way to provide this coverage would be to establish for the internally displaced the equivalent of the High Commissioner for Refugees. The international community would not be prepared to endorse an expensive new organization; but considering that the number of displacements resulting from internal conflicts far exceeds the number of the World War II dislocations in Europe that prompted the establishment of organizations for aiding refugees, the internally displaced people of the world merit at least comparable attention.

If the international community is not prepared or able to make such a major investment, the next best response might be to expand the mandate of the UN High Commissioner for Refugees to explicitly include the internally displaced. Here too, resistance would occur, again because of resource constraints. Enlarging the mandate would require increasing the budget of the organization considerably and expanding the number of its personnel. There would also be the fear that an organization whose specialization and efficiency have become well established might be weakened by the expansion.

A third possible arrangement would be to appoint a senior official within the Secretariat who would be charged with responsibility for the internally displaced. But although the costs would be more manageable, this action would raise questions of jurisdiction and channels of responsibility. An independent unit responsible directly to the secretary-general

15. Special rapporteurs appointed to investigate conditions in particular countries or specific lines of inquiry have provided detailed investigative reports. See, for example, David Weissbrodt, "The Three 'Theme' Special Rapporteurs of the UN Commission on Human Rights," *American Journal of International Law*, vol. 80 (July 1986), pp. 685–98. The working group has traditionally been a mechanism employed by the Commission on Human Rights. See International Commission of Jurists, "An Enlarged UN Commission on Human Rights," *The Review* (June 1992), pp. 62–64.

would be perceived as competing with the Department for Humanitarian Affairs, established in 1992 to coordinate all UN humanitarian activities. But the mandate of the department specifically excludes human rights activities, which were feared to be so politically sensitive that they might jeopardize humanitarian action by the international community. In addition, the department, as it is now designed, is nonoperational: it engages in shaping policy, not in actually rendering field services.

To say that there are difficulties with each of these options is not to rule them out. The challenge is, however, more than one of protecting and assisting the displaced. Viewing their problems in the context of nation building ultimately means addressing the causes of displacement, which in many instances should direct international efforts toward resolving conflicts, ensuring peace and security for all groups and individuals, and guaranteeing equal rights of citizenship without discrimination on the grounds of race, ethnicity, religion, culture, or gender. This is essentially a task for the country concerned and its government. But where the government is not in control or the controlling authority is unable or unwilling to create the conditions necessary to ensure rights, and gross violations of the rights of masses of people result, sovereignty in the sense of responsible government is forfeited and the international community must provide the needed protection and assistance.

Determining the bases for action in specific situations and developing effective enforcement will require major innovations, not only with respect to the legal doctrine and institutional arrangements, but also in the operating principles of international politics and practice. Most of the 25 million people displaced worldwide live under the nominal jurisdictions of governments that are directly or indirectly a primary cause of the human rights violations they experience. Enforcement, therefore, involves the assertive action of the international community to override traditional prerogatives of sovereignty. Such action requires substantial changes in the rules and the conduct of international relations, including changes in the policies of the major Western democracies. Although this is a difficult agenda and one that may seem unduly adventurous, world developments suggest that transcending sovereignty is no longer a forbidden territory for discussion. Contemporary imperatives indeed make such discussion more than an intellectual exercise; it is a matter of life and death for millions.

Reconciling Sovereignty with Responsibility

Protecting and assisting the internally displaced population entails reconciling the possibility of international intervention with traditional concepts of national sovereignty, a problem that increases in direct proportion to the exposure of a country's domestic human rights violations. Representatives of several governments commented in discussions with me that national sovereignty carries with it responsibilities that if not met put a government at risk of forfeiting its legitimacy as the custodian of that sovereignty. One spokesperson for a major power even said, "to put it bluntly, if governments do not live up to those responsibilities," among which he specified the protection of minority rights, "then the international community should intervene, if necessary by force." And it was not only representatives of major powers capable of backing their threat with force who spoke in that vein; similar views were expressed by representatives of African countries who were voicing a global humanitarian concern.

Such pronouncements have almost become truisms that are rapidly making narrow concepts of legality obsolete. When the international community does decide to act, as it did when Iraq invaded Kuwait, when Somalia descended into chaos and starvation, and, albeit less decisively, when the former Yugoslavia disintegrated, controversy about issues of legality becomes futile or of limited value as a brake to guard against precipitous change. Under emergency conditions, speed might indeed be crucial to saving lives.

One observer has recently summarized the new sense of urgency about the need for international response, the ambivalence of the pressures for the needed change, and the pull of traditional legal doctrines:

In the post-Cold War world . . . a new standard of intolerance for human misery and human atrocities has taken hold . . . something quite significant has occurred to raise the consciousness of nations to the plight of peoples within sovereign borders. There is a new commitment—expressed in both moral and legal terms—to alleviate the suffering of oppressed or devastated people. To argue today that norms of sovereignty, non-use of force, and the sanctity of internal affairs are paramount to the collective human rights of people, whose lives and well-being are at risk, is to avoid the hard questions of international law and to ignore the march of history.[16]

The conclusions of a 1992 international conference on human rights protection for internally displaced persons that was attended by human rights specialists, experts from humanitarian organizations, international lawyers, UN and regional organization officials, and government representatives underscored the extent of changes in perspectives on the confrontation between the universal standards of human rights and the parochialism of traditional ideas of sovereignty. The report on the conference states that the "steady erosion" of the concept of absolute sovereignty is making it easier for international organizations, governments, and nongovernmental organizations to intervene when governments refuse to meet the needs of their populations and substantial numbers of people are at risk. The concept of sovereignty, it continues, is becoming understood more in terms of conferring responsibilities on governments to assist and protect persons residing in their territories, so much so that if governments fail to meet their obligations, they risk undermining their legitimacy. The scrutiny of world public opinion as represented by the media makes it difficult for governments to ignore these obligations or defend their failure to act. "Participants considered it essential," the report concludes, "for the international community to continue to 'chip away' and 'pierce' narrow definitions of sovereignty so that sovereignty would not be a barrier to humanitarian intervention."[17]

But to intervene is not an easy choice. Former Secretary-General Javier Perez de Cuellar highlighted the dilemmas when he said in 1991: "We are clearly witnessing what is probably an irresistible shift in public attitudes towards the belief that the defense of the oppressed in the name of morality should prevail over frontiers and legal documents." But he added, "does [intervention] not call into question one of the cardinal principles of international law, one diametrically opposed to it, namely, the obligation of non-interference in the internal affairs of

16. David J. Scheffer, "Toward A Modern Doctrine of Humanitarian Intervention," *University of Toledo Law Review*, vol. 23 (Winter 1992), p. 259.

17. Refugee Policy Group, *Human Rights Protection for Internally Displaced Persons: An International Conference* (Washington, June 1991), p. 7.

States?"[18] In his 1991 annual report, he wrote of the new balance that must be struck between sovereignty and the protection of human rights:

> It is now increasingly felt that the principle of non-interference with the essential domestic jurisdiction of States cannot be regarded as a protective barrier behind which human rights could be massively or systematically violated with impunity. . . . The case for not impinging on the sovereignty, territorial integrity and political independence of States is by itself indubitably strong. But it would only be weakened if it were to carry the implication that sovereignty, even in this day and age, includes the right of mass slaughter or of launching systematic campaigns of decimation or forced exodus of civilian populations in the name of controlling civil strife or insurrection. With the heightened international interest in universalizing a regime of human rights, there is a marked and most welcome shift in public attitudes. To try to resist it would be politically as unwise as it is morally indefensible. It should be perceived as not so much a new departure as a more focused awareness of one of the requirements of peace.

Preferring to avoid confronting the issue of sovereignty, he called for "a higher degree of cooperation and a combination of common sense and compassion," arguing that "we need not impale ourselves on the horns of a dilemma between respect for sovereignty and the protection of human rights. . . . What is involved is not the right of intervention but the collective obligation of States to bring relief and redress in human rights emergencies."[19]

Current Secretary-General Boutros Boutros-Ghali, in his report to the Security Council on strengthening the capacity of the world organization to cope with matters of international peace and security, wrote that respect for sovereignty and integrity is "crucial to any common international progress," but went on to say that "the time of absolute and exclusive sovereignty . . . has passed," that "its theory was never

18. UN press release SG/SM/4560, 24 April 1991. Cited in Gene M. Lyons and Michael Mastanduno, *Beyond Westphalia: International Intervention, State Sovereignty, and the Future of International Society*, (Dartmouth College, 1992) p. 2. Portions of the statement are also cited in Scheffer, "Toward a Modern Doctrine of Humanitarian Intervention," p. 262.

19. J. Perez de Cuellar, *Report of the Secretary-General on the Work of the Organization* (United Nations, 1991), pp. 12, 13.

matched by reality," and that it is necessary for leaders of states "to find a balance between the needs of good internal governance and the requirements of an ever more interdependent world."[20] As one observer commented, "the clear meaning was that governments could best avoid intervention by meeting their obligations not only to other states, but also to their own citizens. If they failed, they might invite intervention."[21]

Because the motives for external intervention may not always be altruistic, a nation's self-interest dictates an appropriate and timely action in self-protection. This was indeed the point made by the secretary-general of the Organization of African Unity, Salim Ahmed Salim, in his bold proposals for an OAU mechanism for conflict prevention and resolution. "If the OAU, first through the Secretary-General and then the Bureau of the Summit, is to play the lead role in any African conflict," he said, "it should be enabled to intervene swiftly, otherwise it cannot be ensured that whoever (apart from African regional organizations) acts will do so in accordance with African interests." Criticizing the tendency to respond only to worst-case scenarios, Salim emphasized the need for preemptive intervention: "The basis for 'intervention' may be clearer when there is a total breakdown of law and order . . . and where, with the attendant human suffering, a spill-over effect is experienced within the neighbouring countries. . . . However, pre-emptive involvement should also be permitted even in situations where tensions evolve to such a pitch that it becomes apparent that a conflict is in the making."[22]

The secretary-general went as far as to suggest that the OAU should take the lead in transcending the traditional view of sovereignty, building on the African values of kinship solidarity and the idea that "every African is his brother's keeper." Considering that "our borders are at best artificial," Salim argued, "we in Africa need to use our own cultural and social relationships to interpret the principle of non-interference in such a way that we are enabled to apply it to our advantage in conflict prevention and resolution."[23] In traditional Africa, third-party intervention for mediation and conciliation is always expected, independently of

20. Boutros-Ghali, *Agenda for Peace*, p. 5.

21. Scheffer, "Toward a Modern Doctrine of Humanitarian Intervention," pp. 262–63.

22. Council of Ministers, *Report of the Secretary-General on Conflicts in Africa: Proposals for an OAU Mechanism for Conflict Prevention and Resolution*, CM/1710 (L.VI) (Adis Ababa, Ethiopia: Organization of African Unity, June 1992), p. 12–13.

23. Council of Ministers, *Report of the Secretary-General*, p. 12.

the will of the parties directly involved in a conflict. Even in domestic disputes, relatives and elders intercede without being invited. "Saving face," which is critical to conflict resolution in Africa, indeed requires that such intervention be unsolicited. But, of course, African concepts and practices under the modern conditions of the nation-state must still balance consideration for state sovereignty with the compelling humanitarian need to protect and assist the dispossessed.

Jan Eliasson, the under secretary-general for humanitarian affairs and emergency relief coordination, stated the way out of the dilemma when, referring to the need for international access to victims of emergencies and mass displacement, he wrote in response to my request for information on the internally displaced: "the consensus in the international community appears to be gradually moving in a new direction. . . . It is basically a question of striking a balance between sovereignty and solidarity with people in need."[24]

Absolute sovereignty is clearly no longer defendable; it never was. The critical question now is under what circumstances the international community is justified to override sovereignty to protect the displaced. The common assumption in international law is that to justify such action there must be a threat to international peace. Some argue that massive violations of human rights and displacement within a country's borders constitute such a threat.[25] Others would contend that a direct threat to international peace is too high a threshold because it would preclude action on too many humanitarian crises. Indeed, they say, the time has come to recognize humanitarian concern as a ground for intervention. Insistence on a threat to international peace as the basis for intervention under chapter VII of the UN Charter has become more a legal fiction than the principle justifying international action.

Thus certain principles are becoming increasingly obvious as policy guidelines. First, sovereignty carries with it moral and material responsibilities for the population. It is from this that the legitimacy of a government derives, whatever the political system or the prevailing ideology. The relationship between the controlling authority and the populace

24. *Comprehensive Study Prepared by Mr. Francis M. Deng, Representative of the Secretary-General on the Human Rights Issues Related to Internally Displaced Persons, Pursuant to Commission on Human Rights Resolution 1992/73,* E/CN.4/1993/35 (United Nations, January 1993).
25. Note by the president of the Security Council, S/25344, February 26, 1993.

should ideally ensure the highest standards of human dignity, but at a minimum it should guarantee food, shelter, physical security, basic health services, and other essentials often denied the internally displaced.

Second, in many countries in which armed conflicts and communal violence cause massive internal displacement, the country is so divided on fundamental issues that legitimacy, and indeed sovereignty, is sharply contested. This is why there is always a strong faction inviting or at least welcoming external intervention. Under those circumstances, the validity of sovereignty must be judged using reasonable standards of how much of the population is represented.

Third, living up to the responsibilities of sovereignty implies a transcendent authority capable of holding the supposed sovereign accountable. Some form of international system has always existed to ensure that states conform to accepted norms or face consequences, whether in the form of unilateral, multilateral, or collective action. Equality among sovereign entities has always been a convenient fiction that has never been backed by realities: some powers have always been more dominant than others and therefore have been explicitly or implicitly charged with the responsibilities of enforcing the agreed norms of behavior.

Fourth, such a role imposes responsibilities on the dominant authority or power leadership that transcend parochialism or exclusive national interests. The responsibilities must serve the broader interests of the community or the collective interest of the human family.

When these principles are translated into practical action in countries torn apart by internal conflicts, a number of implications emerge.

—Sovereignty cannot be an amoral function of authority and control; respect for fundamental human rights must be among its most basic values. Enjoyment of human rights must encompass equitable and effective participation in the political, economic, social, and cultural life of the country, at least as a widely accepted national aspiration. This system of sharing must guarantee individuals and groups that they belong to the nation on an equal footing with the rest of the people, however identified, and that they are sufficiently represented and not discriminated against on the basis of the prevailing views of identity.

—To ensure that these normative goals are met or at least genuinely pursued, the international community as represented by the United Nations is the ideal authority. The imperatives of the power structures and processes may, however, require that this authority be exercised by other powers capable of acting on behalf of the international community. Bilateral and multilateral action may therefore be justified as necessary under certain circumstances.

—Any less collective action should be closely circumscribed to avoid its exploitation for objectives of a more exclusively national character that may erode the transcendent moral authority of global leadership for the good of all humankind.

Although the world is far from a universal government, the foundations, the pillars, and perhaps even the structures of global governance are taking shape with the emergence of a post-cold war international order in which the internally displaced, together with many other dispossessed citizens, are bound to be the beneficiaries. Tearing off the mask of sovereignty to reveal the ugly face of gross violations of human rights is no longer an aspiration but a process that has already started. Governments and other human rights violators are being increasingly scrutinized for such violations. What is now required is to make them fully accountable and to provide international protection and assistance for the victims of human rights violations and unremedied humanitarian tragedies within their domestic jurisdiction. In other words, what is called for is not entirely new but is an intensification and improvement of what has already been unfolding.

Part I

Country Reports

AUSTRIA

HUNGARY

Ljubljana ○
SLOVENIA

○ Zagreb

Subotica ●
Sombor ●

ROMANIA

CROATIA

Vukovay ●

Backa Topola ●

VOJVODINA

● Trnopolje

Banja Luka   Bijelina ●

Batcovic

Belgrade ○

BOSNIA AND
HERCEGOVINA

SERBIA

Sarajevo ○

ADRIATIC
SEA

MONTENEGRO

BULGARIA

Dubrovnik ○   Titograd ○

KOSOVO

ITALY

Skopje ○

MACEDONIA

ALBANIA

GREECE

● CAMPS

1

Yugoslavia: A Nation Dismantled

In the summer of 1991, armed conflict erupted between Serbia and the newly declared Republic of Slovenia, igniting a war that quickly engulfed other Balkan republics in a vortex of interethnic violence. A year later, the postwar Yugoslav state was further dismembered by international recognition of three new states (Slovenia, Croatia, and Bosnia-Herzegovina) and the secession of Macedonia. A redefined Yugoslavia emerged from the union of Serbia and Montenegro, including the provinces of Vojvodina and Kosovo. The war continued unabated and threatened to pull in Bulgaria, Turkey, Albania, and Greece—all of which have ethnic and territorial claims in the region.

In two years more than 200,000 people died and 3.5 million were displaced. In June 1993 some 525,000 of the displaced were said to be in Croatia, 458,000 in Serbia, 33,000 in Slovenia, 2.28 million in Bosnia-Herzeginia (most of whom were Muslims), and 32,000 in Macedonia. Half were inaccessible to aid from the international community. Thousands of others were either wounded or missing in Croatia and Bosnia, the states in which human rights violations were the worst, and untold numbers languished in Serbian and Croatian prisoner-of-war camps.[1]

As the war continues, these numbers are bound to increase. According to the reports of the UN special rapporteur, Helsinki Watch, and other agencies, the human rights abuses in the conflict are particularly deplor-

1. "Rights Meeting Hears Appeal," *New York Times*, June 16, 1993, p. A12; and United Nations High Commissioner for Refugees, "Information Notes on Former Yugoslavia," no. 7/93 (Geneva, June 30, 1993), p. 12.

able because they are carried out in the context of a Serbian policy of "ethnic cleansing"—the summary execution, systematic torture, arbitrary detention, deportation, and forcible displacement of hundreds of thousands of people because of their religion, ethnicity, or nationality. Serbia's goal is to rid all Serbian-controlled areas of non-Serbs or at least decimate their numbers.[2]

Background

Balkan history has been conditioned by expansionist neighbors who have at one time or another forcibly incorporated parts of what became Yugoslavia and who still harbor proprietary sentiments about those regions. Hungary takes a particular interest in the heavily ethnic Hungarian Vojvodina province of Serbia; Austria, perhaps recalling its control under the Hapsburg Empire, assumes a protective attitude toward Slovenia and Croatia; Albania proclaims ethnic solidarity with Albanian-dominated Kosovo; Greece, which historically lays claim to the name of newly independent Macedonia, remains apprehensive; and Turkey, maintaining close diplomatic ties with the Muslims in Bosnia, has attempted to rally the Islamic world in protest against Serbian aggression.

This situation is the outcome of the local particulars of Yugoslav history that have provided the germ of competing nationalist ideologies and ethnic identities. Conflicting concepts of the definition of the Yugoslav state have long plagued the country, creating nationalist tensions that, while intermittently constrained by external pressures, have nevertheless bred two civil wars in this century. A number of scholars have refuted the argument that the conflict stems from centuries of religious and ethnic antagonisms, pointing out that Serbs and Croats lived together in relative peace before the twentieth century.[3] Most, however, recognize the extreme ethnic polarization that fermented in the years before the end of the cold war in the struggle over political power and economic resources.

---

2. Helsinki Watch, *War Crimes in Bosnia-Herzegovina* (New York: Human Rights Watch, August 1992), pp. 63–72; and UN High Commissioner for Refugees, *Emergency Report*, p. 6.

3. For more on this argument see Alex N. Dragnich, *Serbs and Croats: The Struggle in Yugoslavia* (Harcourt Brace Jovanovich, 1992).

The Slavic people migrated to the Balkans from Asia as agrarian settlers and as part of military expeditions as early as the sixth century, maintaining for centuries tribal patterns organized around extended families. These traditional polities were self-governing and decentralized. The South Slavic centralized states and their divergent national identities developed centuries later (though considerably earlier than the era of modern nationalism) as a result of invasions by the Hapsburg Empire in the sixteenth century and the Ottoman Empire in the seventeenth and in resistance to the dual imperialist threat posed by the revival of Hungarian and German nationalism beginning in the late eighteenth century.[4]

Because of these external factors, the founders of the Croatian and Serbian nationalisms developed political outlooks reflecting their separate experiences. At the same time, these events caused both Serbs and Croats to embrace the wider Slavic world in order to preserve the integrity of their nationality. At the beginning of the nineteenth century the Serbians were ruled by the Ottomans and the Croats and Slovenians by the Austro-Hungarian Empire. But by the middle of the century the power of the Ottoman Empire weakened, and the Serbs in Serbia staged a series of successful revolts resulting in a de facto independence that allowed them to develop relatively sophisticated political institutions. In contrast, the Croats and Slovenians, and those Serbians living in their midst, remained in the firm grip of Vienna, which was supported by the great European powers of the day who saw Austro-Hungarian hegemony as a bulwark against Turkish and Russian designs in the Balkans. Serbia's relative autonomy posed a threat in particular to Hapsburg rulers; they responded by sowing seeds of mistrust among the South Slavs, introducing economic and social policies that emphasized the disparities between Croats and Slovenians on the one hand and Serbs on the other.[5] When the Croats and Slovenians emerged from foreign dominion in the early decades of the twentieth century, divergent national visions had already been established. This did not in itself, however, dampen the

4. Ivo Banac, *The National Question in Yugoslavia: Origins, History and Politics* (Cornell University Press, 1984), p. 75

5. By the turn of the century Austria-Hungary felt so threatened by the attraction of its South Slav inhabitants to Serbia that it waged a tariff war, cutting off Serbia's exports to Vienna in order to cripple its economy, and in 1908 it annexed the territory of Bosnia-Herzegovina long claimed by Serbian nationalists. But the real pretext to crush Serbia came in 1914 following the assassination of the heir to the Hapsburg throne, Archduke Franz Ferdinand, in Sarajevo by a Serb.

ardor of the South Slav nationalists who, out of idealism and sheer necessity saw the creation of a common state as their political salvation. Nevertheless, the political expedient upon which the united Yugoslavia was based eventually proved a fatal misunderstanding because the Serbs and Croats each perceived this common state as an extension of their own histories.[6]

The Croats, in seeking to integrate disparate "traditional" Croat lands, developed a diversified form of national consciousness linked to the Roman Catholic faith and saw in a united Yugoslavia a framework for self-determination. As one scholar commented: "Croat flesh instinctively felt too weak in isolation to tackle the fateful problems of liquidating the Turkish occupation [and] bringing down imperial Vienna."[7] In contrast, by the turn of the century Serbian leaders had developed a strictly assimilationist and uniform self-consciousness grounded in the firmly entrenched Orthodox Church of Serbia and hoped to "unite peoples who were the same as themselves in an expanded Serbia."[8] Consequently, the belief that "Yugoslavism meant the respect for the statehood and independence of each South Slavic nation, including the acceptance of minority status where one group was numerically inferior, was not as prevalent among the Serbs as among the Croats."[9] This divergence—the assimilationist character of Serb national ideology versus the integrative nature of Croat national thought—is the rift that eventually led to Yugoslavia's undoing. The fundamental and persistent fact has thus been that the Croats have wanted a separate state, insisting that even though they have never been able to create one, they have never renounced their right to do so. The Serbs, however, have wanted to live in a larger, united, Serbian-dominated state, and Serbia's leadership has been willing to go to war to achieve that objective.[10]

6. Moreover, since Serbs generally lived in four of the South Slav territories (Serbia, Croatia, Bosnia-Herzegovina, and Montenegro) and the Croats in three (Serbia, Croatia, and Bosnia-Herzegovina) the idea of one state could not serve as a unifying factor, particularly within the context of divergent historical experiences. Language (Serbo-Croatian), the chief common denominator that helped to give birth to a unified Yugoslav state, was thus ultimately insufficient in facilitating unification.

7. Banac, *National Question in Yugoslavia*, p. 70.

8. James Gow, "Deconstructing Yugoslavia" *Survival*, vol. 33 (July–August 1991), p. 292.

9. Banac, *National Question in Yugoslavia*, p. 75.

10. Vladimir Oligorov, "Is What I Left Right?" Uppsala University, Uppsala, Sweden, p. 14.

The first Yugoslav (the name means South Slav) constitution, drafted in 1921, was relatively democratic but was not federalist. It was passed by the dominant Serbian parties; in opposition the Croatian and Slovenian parties desired regional autonomy. This hastily drawn unifying instrument created a strongly centralized government based in Belgrade that was increasingly used by the Serbs to impose unequal taxation and to pass legislation that discriminated on the basis of language and national identity. On occasion Belgrade confiscated lands from other ethnic groups and turned them over to Serbian colonists.[11] Therein lies the genesis of the Yugoslav national problem that has helped to bring about the demise of two incarnations of Yugoslavia. The first Yugoslavia failed because its national vision, dominated by the Serbs, suppressed the aspirations for self-determination harbored by the other South Slavs. National animosities erupted in a many-sided civil war during the Second World War until the communists led by Josip Broz Tito defeated the German forces in 1945.[12]

For nearly forty years after World War II a loose amalgamation of six republics and two autonomous provinces, renamed the Federal People's Republic of Yugoslavia, was a regionally pluralistic arrangement, forcibly held together by the authoritarian communist regime of President Tito. Tito's falling out with the Soviet Union engendered a precarious state of national unity, a unity buttressed by Yugoslavia's leadership among the nonaligned nations. But any vision of a South Slav nation-state in the modern European sense of the term proved a chimera. Serbs predominated in the military officer corps, the Belgrade bureaucracy, and the secret police. Attempting to curb Serb dominance, Tito, himself of Slovenian-Croatian descent, redrew regional geographic lines that left one-third of all Serbs as minorities in other republics.[13] Meanwhile, a deteriorating economy contributed to genuine democratization but also increased fragmentation as "new associations and groupings emerged, many with clear political programs. Some of the founders of these

11. Sabrina Petra Ramet, "War in the Balkans," *Foreign Affairs*, vol. 71 (Fall 1992), p. 81.

12. In 1941 Germany invaded Yugoslavia and created an independent Croatian state unleashing a vicious tribal war in the process. The leaders of Croatia perpetuated genocide against Serbs, Jews, and Gypsies; Serb nationalists responded by massacring Croats and especially Bosnian Muslims, many of whom had allied themselves with the fascist regime in Croatia.

13. Josef Joffe, "Bosnia: The Return of History," *Commentary*, October 1992, p. 25.

associations eventually assumed positions of leadership in Slovenia, Croatia, Bosnia, and Macedonia."[14]

Historical insecurities exacerbated by the faltering economy motivated elites to increasingly manipulate nationalist, rather than communist, sentiments to gain political legitimacy, rekindling sensitive historical disputes in the process. Slovenia and Croatia, in particular, demanded and received a greater degree of political autonomy from Belgrade. Separatist sentiments became more pronounced in the wake of the economic crisis of the 1980s, which saw an across-the-board deterioration in the standard of living characterized by a surge in unemployment and hyperinflation and made worse by a series of IMF stabilization measures designed to promote exports in Western markets.[15] In 1986 in the wake of anti-Serb riots in outlying republics, the Serbian Academy of Sciences and Arts drew up a memorandum spelling out an ultranationalist program that called for meeting the threat of the state's disintegration with uncompromising force. For many Serbs the specter of state disintegration threatened the vision of a Serbian-dominated state. The only solution seemed to lie in reviving the mythology of a Greater Serbia. This revival began in earnest in 1987 following a coup within the Serbian party that brought to power communist Slobodan Milosevic, elected because of his support for the program advocated in the academy memorandum.

By 1991 Yugoslavia could no longer be held together. The collapse of Soviet hegemony in Eastern Europe in 1989 had removed the threat of an external enemy. And the communist assurances of South Slav solidarity evaporated when Slovenia and Croatia seceded from the federation in June. The secession, supported by Germany and Austria, awakened a host of ethnic animosities. Croatia had been a fascist state allied with Nazi Germany in World War II and had waged a genocidal war against the Serbs. In addition, the pattern of alliances of Western European nations, in which Germany and Austria appeared to side with the Croats and France, Britain, and the United States with the Serbs, replayed the politics of the two world wars, a pattern that may have paralyzed attempts at

---

14. Ramet, "War in the Balkans," p. 82.

15. See Branko Milanovic, *Poverty in Poland, Hungary, and Yugoslavia in the Years of Crisis, 1978–87*, PRE working paper 507 (Washington: World Bank, September 1990).

intervention or measures that might have prevented conflict.[16] Finally, with international recognition of Croatia and the other republics, Serbia confronted the question of where its borders would be drawn and what was to be done with Bosnia, which had a minority population of 31.5 percent Serbs (Serbs made up 11.6 percent of the population of Croatia and a minuscule portion of the population of Slovenia).[17] The solution seemed to be to carve out a Greater Serbia.

By the beginning of 1992, as the conflict raged and abuses of human rights of Bosnian Muslims escalated, the United Nations and European Community were able to bring enough pressure to bear to force Belgrade and its Serbian proxy militias in Bosnia to agree to a peace plan based on the establishment of ten autonomous regions in a federated Bosnia. But by then, Serbian militias controlled one-fifth of Croatia and two-thirds of Bosnia, and their leaders demonstrated no inclination to relinquish the territory.[18] Meanwhile the Croats had prepared a counteroffensive against the non-Croatian usurpers of their land, and the fighting was undiminished. A year later, amid increasing gains by the Serbs and Croats in Bosnia, the chief European negotiator in the war, Lord David Owen, was forced to pronounce his own peace plan a failure and urged the Muslims in Bosnia to "make the best of what has happened on the ground." Accepting a proposal made by the Serbs and Croats and speaking on behalf of the European Community as well as the United Nations, Lord Owen called for the division of Bosnia-Herzegovina along ethnic lines and its partition into separate Serbian, Croatian, and Muslim states—effectively conceding to the Serbs and Croats their nationalist dreams.[19]

Observations

Violations of human rights in the former Yugoslavia have been documented in detail by Tadeusz Mazowiecki following two visits there.

16. For a discussion of Balkan history during World War II see Dragnich, *Serbs and Croats*, and Banac, *National Question in Yugoslavia*. For the failure to prevent Serbian aggression see Joffe, "Bosnia: The Return of History," p. 29.

17. Ramet, "War in the Balkans," p. 81.

18. John F. Burns, "Hemming and Hawing, Bosnia's Serbs Back Peace," *New York Times*, January 21, 1993, p. A3.

19. Paul Lewis, "Balkan Negotiator, in Shift, Backs Plan Dividing Bosnia," *New York Times*, June 18, 1993, p. A28.

Mazowiecki was appointed UN special rapporteur on the basis of resolution 1992/S-1/1, which the Commission on Human Rights adopted at its first special session on August 14, 1992. The resolution states that the commission was "appalled at the continuing reports of widespread, massive, and grave violations of human rights perpetrated within the territory of the former Yugoslavia, especially in Bosnia and Herzegovina." It expressed "particular abhorrence" at the concept and practice of ethnic cleansing, carried out mostly by Serbs, which "at a minimum entails deportations and forcible removal or expulsion of persons from their homes in flagrant violation of their human rights, and which is aimed at the dislocation or destruction of ethnic, racial or religious groups." The special rapporteur was mandated "to investigate first hand the human rights situation in the territory of the former Yugoslavia, in particular within Bosnia and Herzegovina, and to receive relevant, credible information on the human rights situation there from governments, individuals, intergovernmental and nongovernmental organizations, on a continuing basis, and to avail himself or herself of the assistance of existing mechanisms of the Commission on Human Rights."[20]

Following his first visit in August 1992, Mazowiecki reported that "most of the territory of the former Yugoslavia, in particular Bosnia and Herzegovina, is at present the scene of massive and systematic violations of human rights, as well as grave violations of humanitarian law. Ethnic cleansing is the cause of most such violations." The report went on to state that "discrimination, harassment, and maltreatment of ethnic Serbs are also serious and widespread problems in Croatia." Although acknowledging that the Muslims have been accused of pursuing a deliberate policy of emptying the territory under their control of ethnic Serbs, the report concluded, as a result of Mazowiecki's visit to a Muslim-controlled area in Bosnia and Herzegovina, that no policy that could be compared with ethnic cleansing was being carried out in this area.[21]

In October Mazowiecki invited me in my capacity as the special representative of the secretary-general on internally displaced persons,

20. UN Commission on Human Rights resolution 1992/S-1/1, E/CN.4 (Geneva, August 14, 1992).
21. United Nations, *Report on the Situation in the Territory of the Former Yugoslavia by Mr. Tadeusz Mazowiecki*, E/CN.4/1992/S-1/9 (Geneva, August 28, 1992), pp. 2, 5. Hereafter first Mazowiecki report.

along with the special rapporteurs on extrajudicial, summary, or arbitrary executions and on torture, the chairman of the Working Group on Arbitrary Detention, and medical and forensic experts, to assist him on a second mission. Using Belgrade and Zaghreb as bases, I visited Batcovic and Bijelina in Bosnia and, in Serbia, Backa Topola (near Sombor) and Subotica in Vojvodina. I also accompanied Mazowiecki to Banja Luka, Trnopolje, and Sarajevo in Bosnia and Herzegovina and, together with the other members of the delegation, Vukovar, a city in eastern Croatia almost entirely destroyed by shelling during the November 1991 attack by the Yugoslav army.

Mazowiecki's second report concluded that "Grave and massive violations of human rights continue to occur in the territory of the former Yugoslavia. The military conflict in Bosnia and Herzegovina, which is aimed at achieving 'ethnic cleansing,' remains a matter of particular and most urgent concern." The report went on to say that since the first visit, "widespread and serious human rights violations continue to be committed in Bosnia and Herzegovina and in certain respects have intensified . . . [and] a great number of people are suffering and have lost their lives. Thousands more find their lives threatened and their human dignity violated. Unless immediate action is taken, many of them will not survive winter.[22]

The genocidal implication of this tragic war was alluded to in resolution 1992/S-2/1, adopted by the Commission on Human Rights at its second special session, which called upon states "to consider the extent to which the acts committed in Bosnia and Herzegovina and in Croatia constitute genocide, in accordance with the Convention on the Prevention and Punishment of the Crime of Genocide."[23] Ethnic cleansing is a close kin of genocide. The means used by an ethnic group in control of a given territory to force another ethnic group from the territory include threats, harassment and intimidation, rape, torture, extrajudicial execution, and shooting or using explosives against homes and places of business, destroying places of worship and cultural importance, and forcibly relocating populations. The ethnic Serbs in de facto control of

22. United Nations, *Report on the Situation in the Territory of the Former Yugoslavia by Mr. Tadeusz Mazowiecki,* E/CN.4/1992/S-1/10 (Geneva, October 27, 1992), p. 1. Hereafter second Mazowiecki report.

23. UN Commission on Human Rights resolution 1992/S-2/1.

certain areas of Bosnia and Herzegovina and the UN protected areas are primarily responsible for the ethnic cleansing there. As Mazowiecki noted, "although human rights violations are being perpetrated by all parties to the conflicts" and there are victims on both sides, "the situation of the Muslim population is particularly tragic; they feel that they are threatened with extermination."[24]

The Serbs do not of course consider themselves the main perpetrators of violence and rights violations. In discussions in Serbian camps, Serbian refugees delivered a litany of human rights abuses by the Muslims. In one area Serbian authorities presented a long list of detention centers in which Muslims kept 1,500 Serbs of all ages, including babies and people as old as age ninety. They said some centers had gone months without food. They also said a Serb had been knifed to death and beheaded. Many people were said to be detained in villages.

Serbian military authorities explained their violence against non-Serbs as a reaction to the dismantling of their country by the international community, which, they claimed, sought to foster an ethnically based concept of nationhood. Their bitterness at the dismemberment and the UN-imposed sanctions was intense. Some explained the war in Bosnia and Herzegovina as a struggle for the survival of their Serbian identity and their freedom from Muslim domination.

My visits to detention camps in Batcovic and Trnopolje in Bosnia, which are controlled by ethnic Serbs, dramatically demonstrated the discriminatory attitude of the Serbs toward Muslims and other non-Serbs. The Batcovic camp was said to be among the best in Bosnia and Herzegovina. For that reason the Serbian authorities preferred to call it a center and not a camp, and indeed, the detainees did not complain of ill-treatment. They had a clinic with a medical officer and looked mostly healthy and well-fed. Some questioned having one-third to one-half of the detainees forced to work in the fields, but they seemed to accept the authorities' explanation that their labor was both needed and good for them, since it killed time and gave them exercise. But they were appallingly crowded—about a thousand men (initially 1,373) were herded into two unheated barns or stables, with blanket-covered hay to sleep on. Winter was fast approaching and there was no prospect of heating in sight. The de facto Serbian authorities asserted that the detainees had

24. First Mazowiecki report, 1992/S-1/9, p. 12.

actually been, or were about to become, involved in combat when they were seized. However, all the detainees claimed to be civilians who had been rounded up for unknown reasons.

In the "refugee" camp for Serbians at Backa Topola in Vojvodina, conditions contrasted sharply. The refugees were accommodated in an artists' colony where, in groups of several people, they slept in individual rooms on beds with mattresses and bedding and ate in a pleasant dining room with very good food prepared in a clean, well-kept modern kitchen. Although their rooms were congested and they complained bitterly about the atrocities of the war and the brutal treatment they had received, their living conditions, if by no means normal, were relatively comfortable.

The authorities in Backa Topolo explained the situation of the Serbian refugees in a way that shed light on the interethnic dynamics involved. The refugees went through three stages. During the first stage, they were well received and accommodated by the local population, often living as guests in families. During the second stage, the hardships of the situation forced the families to ask the refugees to leave. At the third stage, the refugees, desperate for accommodation, began to break into homes. Were they breaking into the homes of non-Serbs and forcing them out? I wondered later but had no answer. However, the contrast between initial receptivity to refugees and the eventual disenchantment and hostility of the local population was ominous in that it set the stage for the "ethnic cleansing" to come.

Conditions in the Trnopolje camp (which I visited jointly with Mazowiecki) were shocking. More than 3,000 men, women, and children (Muslims and Croats hoping to flee ethnic cleansing) were packed into three unheated buildings. Our delegation arrived at the camp on a cold, rainy day that only aggravated their hardships. The detainees slept on blankets spread out on cement floors. They had very little to eat and were subject to harassment and violence. Mazowiecki wrote in his second report that the people

live in unspeakable squalor, sleeping on thin blankets and lice-infested straw, drinking contaminated water and surviving on minimum rations of bread. Some of these persons have remained in this camp for more than four months. The physician accompanying the Special Rapporteur stated that upper respiratory infection was spreading like wildfire.

Children and adults were suffering from diarrhea, presumably from contaminated water and near-total absence of sanitation. There are diabetics without insulin, heart patients without digitalis, and persons suffering from hypertension without medication.[25]

Just as conditions of the Muslim detainees at Batcovic had differed from those of the refugee center at Backa Topola, so did conditions at the Trnopolje camp contrast with those of a Serbian-run center in Banja Luka, Bosnia-Herzegovina, where Serbian "refugees"—in fact displaced persons of Serbian origin—slept on beds with mattresses and linen and ate three meals a day in dining room furnished with cloth-covered tables. Their children, well fed and well dressed, attended school. The Serbian authorities had complained that international visitors were neglecting to observe centers for Serbian refugees and displaced persons and insisted on our including that center in the program. The decision of the de facto Serbian authorities to show the center despite thereby exposing the huge disparity between living conditions at the two camps was attributed by some observers to the difference between the standards the Serbs regard as appropriate for members of their own ethnic group and the standards considered appropriate for Muslims.

In the town of Subotica in Vojvodina, the mayor and leaders of Hungarians, Croats, Ukrainians, and Slovaks gave detailed accounts of discriminatory Serb policies—in employment, for instance, especially in police and administrative posts—and acts of intimidation aimed at forcing them to leave. They predicted the development of communal violence and civil disorder.

It must always be remembered that behind the faceless statistics of the masses victimized by these tragedies are individual men, women, and children. In Bijelina a Muslim whom the Serbs displayed as a symbol of the interethnic and interreligious solidarity of the community and who had publicly reaffirmed that solidarity disclosed a totally different version of the situation in a confidential interview. He described in detail the harassment, intimidation, and violence to which the Muslims were subjected and pleaded for help in returning home, notwithstanding the dangers there.

---

25. Second Mazowiecki report, 1992/S-1/10, pp. 3-4.

In another interview a Serb bragged that he was occupying the house of a Muslim living in Switzerland who had entrusted him with the care of the property. He offered this as evidence of the solidarity between ethnic groups in the area. But he later confessed that the Muslim owner had fled the country, thus unwittingly revealing the popular Serbian tactic of intimidating homeowners until they vacate their homes, which are then occupied by Serbs.

In the Trnopolje camp a young woman stepped forward to report that she had been raped several times by the Serbs. Rape was mentioned by many witnesses, including the leader of the Muslim community in Sarajevo, as a common offence against Muslims. Also in Trnopolje an elderly mother, with the help of several people, struggled to contain her son, a young man who was experiencing an epileptic seizure. She explained that he had been under medication but was out of medicine.

Desperate as people in the camps were, many saw in our mission a symbol of hope to which they clung with gripping hands, some with tears in their eyes. But some sat or lay in dispassionate or apathetic helplessness and hopelessness. Between those two perspectives lie the prospects for their future.

Our UN visit in Sarajevo comprised meetings with leaders of Muslim, Catholic, and Jewish communities and with the Council of the Presidency. The Jewish leader summarized the situation when he told the delegation that no human principle was respected in the conflict and that whatever help they needed was probably already too late. Emphasizing the destruction of cultural monuments, he predicted that when the conflict ended, Sarajevo would be a desert and that those who survived would be devoid of culture or human values because people were dying in their souls. And yet, the last words in the meeting with members of the presidency were "Please, please, help us."

Particularly ironic was that religious differences were given an intrinsically ethnic significance that separated people of the same race and ethnicity into very different identity groups. Observers, including Serbs who did not identify with either side of the conflict, said that people of mixed families were particularly vulnerable and were in some instances traumatized by the schisms. And there were some who still saw themselves as Yugoslavs and refused to be identified otherwise. The level of interethnic hatred and brutality emphasized the sharp cleavages that divided people who until recently had been citizens of one state and who had offered pluralistic countries a model of diversity within unity. Ethnic animosities have opened historical wounds and transformed the democratic model into dystopia.

The former Yugoslavia is a telling example of a country in which displacement is inextricably intertwined with general civil conflict. Although it is urgent to identify, protect, and assist the displaced, the reliable solution to their problem is a comprehensive resolution of that conflict. The internally displaced are the most adversely affected of a much larger population that also suffers from civil strife, communal violence, and violations of human rights. Any measures to protect and assist this general population should also be conceived within the framework of an encompassing strategy that addresses the roots of a national crisis.

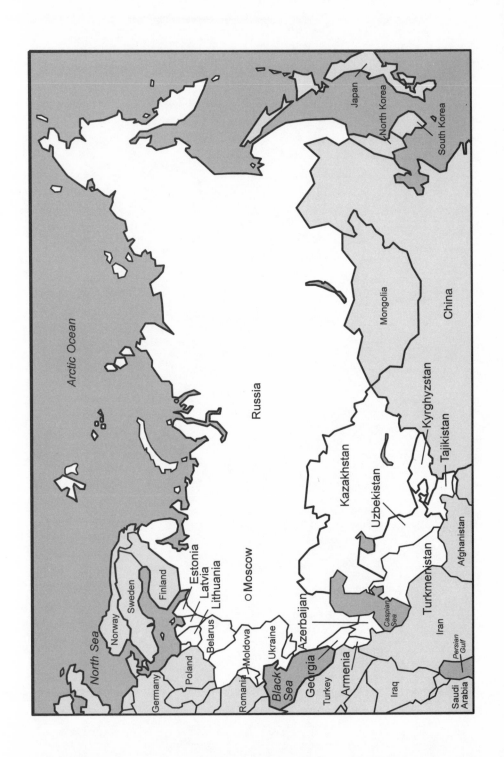

2

Russia:
A Crisis in the Making

Although crises may have displaced more than 1 million persons in the
Russian Federation and created 400,000 refugees, a situation that poses
serious challenges to protection and assistance efforts, what concerns
officials are the even worse crises predicted in the federation and in other
republics of the former Soviet Union that are now independent states.
Ethnic divisions and rivalries long suppressed by the Soviet regime have
surfaced in a number of regions. In Armenia and Azerbaijan, fierce fighting has forcibly displaced thousands. In the Asian republics of the federation, ethnic Russians who settled in the past century are suddenly finding
themselves unwanted. Not since Stalin's purges in the 1930s have displaced persons and refugees posed such a grave threat in the region.

Throughout the former Soviet Union, governments' struggles to hold
on to power against increasingly insistent political opposition or to
preserve territorial integrity in the face of separatist forces have precipi-
tated armed conflicts. As a result, according to a 1992 study commissioned by the U.S. Agency for International Development, Russia alone
may have received 200,000 refugees, and as many as 400,000 migrants
voluntarily left the Transcaucasian and central Asian republics and the
Baltic states by the end of 1992. A Refugee Policy Group report has
estimated that perhaps 300,000 people left Kyrgyzstan, Tadjikistan,
Turkmenistan, and Uzbekistan in 1990.[1]

1. U.S. Agency for International Development, *Report by the Emergency Humanitarian Assessment Team in the New Independent States* (Washington, June 1992); and
Refugee Policy Group, *Migration in and from Central and Eastern Europe: Addressing
the Root Causes* (Washington, June 1992).

All in all, the dissolution of the Soviet Union has exposed 65 million former Soviet citizens living outside their republics of origin to the possibility of displacement. The largest number—25 million—are ethnic Russians who have found themselves aliens overnight, discriminated against in lands they have called home for generations, particularly in Moldova, the Baltic states, and the central Asian republics. Peoples in those states often resent the Russians as usurpers who have discriminated against their languages and cultures: reverse discrimination appears to be the new order of things. Some newly independent states, most notably Ukraine, have adopted a relatively inclusive attitude toward nonindigenous minorities, guaranteeing all ethnic groups equal political rights and the freedom to use their languages, but it remains to be seen whether this tolerance will withstand pervasive socioeconomic pressures.[2]

Background

Although interethnic hostilities resulting from racial, religious, and socioeconomic differences were widespread in eighteenth- and nineteenth-century Russia, government policy under the czars approached the problems in a manner far different from that employed by the Soviet regime. In the tradition of other European empires, the Russian Empire encouraged indirect rule, which usually involved alternately applying force and granting concessions to control the various ethnic and national groups, a process that left the social structures of the conquered peoples mostly intact. The czars were "content to subjugate [the groups] and extract their loyalty, to coopt part of the indigenous elite as a means of establishing indirect rule, and to pursue these peoples' assimilation by means of long-term administrative adaptation and migration."[3]

Current regional and ethnic tensions are mostly the result of the seven decades of Soviet power that followed the Bolshevik Revolution. Despite

2. See the Ukrainian parliament's "Declaration on the Rights of Nationalities of the Ukraine," November 1991, in Foreign Broadcast Information Service, *Daily Report: Soviet Union*, November 5, 1991, p. 63. There are reports, however, that in some educational institutions Ukrainian authorities have already violated the principles of ethnic and linguistic tolerance spelled out by the parliament.

3. Gerhard Simon, *Nationalism and Policy Toward the Nationalities in the Soviet Union: From Totalitarian Dictatorship to Post-Stalinist Society*, trans. Karen Foster and Oswald Foster (Boulder, Colo.: Westview Press, 1991), p. 3. Soviet ideology was also convinced of its integrative nature and theorized that the rivalries of nationalities could be resolved within the context of the socialist revolution, which would merge like-minded peoples with the state.

its Marxist-Leninist canon, which was supposed to ensure the elimination of national, racial, and religious animosities it attributed to the divisive bourgeois policies of the czars, an increasingly centralized state controlled by the Communist party employed a style of governance reminiscent of that used by the harsher colonial powers. The Soviet state thus exacerbated the enmities of ethnic groups that eventually provided the greatest impetus for the decolonization that would demolish it.[4]

The ethnic and national rivalries were first revived in the 1930s by Josef Stalin's policy of collectivization (the formation of large state-owned farms), which contrasted sharply with most policies of the pre-revolutionary Russian state. In Ukraine, collectivization was designed to serve two objectives: to confiscate as much grain as possible from the peasant population, regardless of the cost, so as to finance the ambitious Soviet industrial revolution, and to make an example of the Ukrainian peasant who, Stalin believed, represented the "national question"—efforts to secede from the Soviet Union and movements opposing the Communist party.[5]

The result of this policy, which involved the wholesale slaughter of livestock, the deportation of hundreds of thousands of people, and mass executions, was to bring about a famine that may have left 6 million dead in the course of only two years (1932–33).[6] It was a tragedy that created deep and enduring social, psychological, political, and demographic scars. Nor was Ukraine the only region to suffer. During World War II, Soviet authorities forcibly relocated millions of non-Russians—Volga Germans, Crimean Tartars, Chechens, Ingush, Kalmyks—presumably to punish them for collaborating with Germany.

Dispersing populations that could have formed a core of resistance was but one way of attempting to preserve Soviet hegemony. The Kremlin also systematically stirred conflicts among ethnic groups to fragment any drive toward self-determination or independence.[7] Violent

---

4. Simon, *Nationalism and Policy*, p. 6. Although Russian nationalism was often used as a convenient tool of centralization, many Soviet leaders after Lenin were not of pure Russian stock. Josef Stalin (his real name was Dzhugashvili), who revitalized the Russification movement, was ethnic Georgian; Nikita Khrushchev, Leonid Brezhnev, and Constantine Chernenko had Ukrainian roots.

5. Orest Subtelny, *Ukraine: A History* (University of Toronto Press, 1988), pp. 415–16.

6. Subtelny, *Ukraine*, p. 413.

7. Roger Winter, "Chips off the Old Bloc: Displacement in a Disintegrating USSR," *World Refugee Survey—1992* (Washington: U.S. Committee for Refugees, 1992), p. 78.

attacks against traditional social structures undermined the economic foundations of societies in the Soviet east. And as early as the 1920s the regime encouraged large migrations of ethnic Russians to non-Russian territories, especially the Baltic states and the central Asian republics, a policy intended to plant loyal colonists to enforce Soviet law and dilute the homogeneity of the indigenous populations.[8]

Although the results took a long time to manifest themselves, the policies in many ways boomeranged. Attempts to eradicate traditional cultures met with stubborn if subdued resistance. Tribal structures and Islamic culture, for example, persisted despite the assimilation policies.[9] Forced migrations and fomented ethnic conflicts may have had an atomizing effect, but they also engendered resurgent nationalist aspirations and formidable socioeconomic grievances. This result was reinforced by the ethnic Russian migrations. Many colonists did not integrate with the local cultures and societies and did not learn the local languages. Yet they held the key positions in the state bureaucracy, industries, and the military, which fueled resentment.

Nevertheless, the Soviets held the system together for more than seventy years. Ironically, this success as well as the ultimate disintegration of the state probably owed more to a relatively late policy— Moscow's distribution of social and political concessions—than to the persistent harrying of traditional cultures that was characteristic of the Soviet Union's earlier years. The concessions facilitated a direct albeit precarious link between authorities at the center and their elite proxies in the periphery that encouraged some social cohesiveness. But at the same time, the policy allowed for an increasingly energetic decolonization movement that destroyed the empire.[10]

8. Between 1959 and 1989, for example, the ethnic Russians in Lithuania, Latvia, and Estonia increased 48.9 percent, 62.9 percent, and 97.9 percent, respectively. Lubomyr Hajda and Mark Beissinger, eds., *The Nationalities Factor in Soviet Politics and Society* (Boulder, Colo.: Westview Press, 1990), p. 54.

9. Although the religiosity in the Muslim republics of central Asia has remained comparatively high, there is some debate over the relative importance of religious identity and ethnic or tribal affiliation. For some scholars, violent interethnic conflicts in recent years would seem to suggest ethnic loyalties have primacy over supranational Islamic ties. See, for instance, James Critchlow, "Islam in Soviet Central Asia: Renaissance or Revolution?" *Religion in Communist Lands*, vol. 18 (Autumn 1990), p. 208.

10. As late as the 1960s and early 1970s many Soviet and Western scholars were convinced that acculturation, particularly among the soviet elites, was irreversible. See Simon, *Nationalism and Policy*, p. 7.

On paper, these concessions granted all Soviet citizens legal equality, permitted linguistic and territorial autonomy, and, although insisting on state unity, applied a federal constitutional structure. In practice, however, the loosening of the system allowed the promotion of national languages and the rise of non-Russian literature and media that, in combination with higher levels of modernization exemplified by an expanded educational system, resulted in a new intelligentsia prepared to assume leadership positions after independence.[11] Within the context of a shrinking Soviet economy plagued by hyperinflation, food shortages, and a spiraling debt burden, these factors—in addition to resurgent religious institutions—promoted the new elite's aspirations for independence. In the late 1960s and throughout the 1970s, protests erupted and assumed distinct nationalist overtones, particularly in Ukraine and the Baltic states.[12] In what would prove a fatal lack of "new thinking," Moscow met the protestors with repressions reminiscent of the Stalin years, resulting in hundreds of deaths, inflaming anti-Russian sentiments, and reinforcing ethnic hostilities. "The sources of the existing situation," one Soviet official would write later, "are found in the complex . . . problems arising from the distortion of the nationality policy during the periods of the cult of personality and stagnation."[13]

Thus upon assuming power in 1985, Mikhail Gorbachev inherited not only the twin curses of economic deterioration and general political stalemate but also a nationality problem that was the outgrowth of the very policies of social mobilization and ideological indoctrination intended to eliminate it. Gorbachev chose to concentrate on the economic and political problems. When he launched his policy of perestroika, or political reform, he clearly could not have foreseen that he would unleash stubborn forces of democratization and decentralization in the process.

The turning point came with the March 1989 elections for the Congress of People's Deputies that Gorbachev hoped to use as a mandate with which to pursue his gradualist policies with greater vigor and

11. After the Khrushchev era many non-Russians even enjoyed extensive control of their local administrations and economies. Simon, *Nationalism and Policy*, p. 4.

12. Bohdan Nahaylo and Victor Swoboda, *Soviet Disunion: A History of the Nationalities Problem in the USSR* (Macmillan, 1990), pp. 249-53.

13. Adam B. Ulam, "Looking at the Past: The Unraveling of the Soviet Union," *Current History* (October 1992), p. 340.

confidence. Instead, the election results (especially in Moscow and Leningrad) constituted a wholesale repudiation of the entire communist system as many party bosses lost their seats to antiestablishment politicians, the most notable of whom was Boris Yeltsin. The election results spelled the end of the Communist party's domination of Soviet politics and portended the resurgence and ultimate victory of separatist and nationalist forces. Moreover, because the diffusion of political power was accompanied by a new consensus affirming pursuit of a free market economy, Gorbachev could hardly turn to the harsh authoritarian policies of earlier years. "No sooner did the rulers of the Soviet Union explicitly abandon the mission to remake the world in a Marxist-Leninist image than power began to slip out of their hands. With communism no longer able to sustain the fiction that it was the wave of the future, the Communist party could no longer act as the glue which held the multinational state together."[14]

The disintegration of the Soviet Union was accelerated by the aborted coup of August 19–21, 1991, staged by a small group of reactionaries who sought to forestall the imminent signing of a new Treaty of the Union that would have radically transferred power from the central government to the republics. "The coup's attempt to reassert central control by force greatly undermined the credibility of the center; its humiliating failure fatally undermined the center's authority."[15] In subsequent months the collapse of central authority became official as Gorbachev resigned and the Communist party was formally dissolved. By that time domestic and international pressures encouraged the leaders of the republics to insist that the Union Treaty be renegotiated, reducing central authority further and accelerating nationalist sentiments. This demand led to the immediate independence of Estonia, Latvia, and Lithuania. Most of the other republics, including Ukraine, followed suit. By December 1991, all that could be salvaged from the wreckage of empire was the hastily drawn and loose Commonwealth of Independent States that included all the former Soviet republics except the three Baltic states, which chose not to join, and Georgia, which was sliding into civil war and was excluded.

14. Ulam, "Looking at the Past," p. 344.
15. Stuart D. Goldman, *Post-Soviet Transformation* (Congressional Research Service, January 1992), p. 3.

Predictably, as political power moved from the center to the outlying republics, historical, ethnic, and political conflicts erupted. Struggles raged between Armenians and Azeris over control of Nagorno Karabakh, an enclave of Armenians in Azerbaijan. The conflict, which threatens to have wide-ranging regional implications, has displaced 256,000 persons, according to the UN High Commissioner for Refugees (the U.S. Committee for Refugees estimates one-half million, with 1,000 deaths in recent years). The Russian-speaking population and the armed forces of the hard-line nationalist communist leaders of Moldova are at odds over the trans-Dniester region, a small strip of Moldova adjacent to Ukraine, where Helsinki Watch estimates one in five people (approximately 100,000) have been displaced.[16] Muslim revivalists in Tadjikistan are arrayed against old communists, a conflict, according to the U.S. Committee for Refugees, that has contributed to the internal displacement of 250,000 Tadjiks and the potential displacement of 300,000 ethnic Russians who still live in the republic. According to Helsinki Watch, "in all of these armed conflicts, parties [have] frequently violated rules of war intended to protect noncombatants set out by articles of the Geneva Convention pertaining to internal armed conflicts. In addition, human rights abuses range from attacks on civilians and civilian structures, to the indiscriminate use of land mines, as well as acts of discrimination, including dismissals from work on the basis of ethnic origin and political conviction."[17]

Because of various other trouble spots, the numbers of refugees and internally displaced persons will escalate. According to the report commissioned by the U.S. Agency for International Development, Tatarstan, Chechen-Ingush, Abkhazia, and parts of Siberia are discussing secession from existing political entities. Recently, thousands have demanded the resignation of communist leaders in Kazakhstan; Georgian soldiers have clashed with South Ossetians who fear Georgian hegemony; and a dis-

16. The Russian-speaking population includes some ethnic Moldovans and Ukrainians.
17. Human Rights Watch, *Helsinki Watch Annual Report 1992* (Washington, 1992). Other figures compiled from UN High Commissioner for Refugees, *Displaced in the Balkans* (Geneva, 1992); and U.S. Committee for Refugees, *Tadjikistan Update* (Washington, 1992). For details regarding human rights abuses in Nagorno Karabakh, see Helsinki Watch, *Bloodshed in the Caucasus: Escalation of the Armed Conflict in Nagorno Karabakh* (Washington: Human Rights Watch, September 1992).

pute over the Crimea is tightening already difficult tensions between Ukraine and Russia.[18] Perhaps more troubling for Russia—for ethnic reasons—is the enmity brewing in the Baltic states. Particularly in Estonia, Russians are "contemplating abandoning their homes in very large numbers . . . partly because these republics have passed what [the Russians] perceive to be discriminatory language laws requiring residents to speak the indigenous language to hold certain jobs and/or obtain citizenship."[19]

Observations

During my visit to the Russian Federation in November 1992 I had extensive discussions with the authorities on the problems of displaced persons and refugees. The officials were unusually candid about the internal problems of their country. As the head of the Federal Migration Service said, "There is nothing to hide." Tracing the causes of displacement and migration to ethnic conflicts, especially in the late 1980s, she predicted the conflicts would continue and intensify, with forced migration perhaps stabilizing in 1994. The situation in Russia, she contended, was more complex than anywhere else in the world, including the former Yugoslavia, because of the history of overbearing relations with the former republics. She urged that the study undertaken by the special representative of the secretary-general be frank and realistic in addressing the problem.

Although she agreed with the main elements of the definition of the internally displaced in the UN analytical report on them, she distinguished between the international and local variants of the definition, stressing that in the Russian context, displaced persons of Russian nationality, which could be granted to any citizen of the former Soviet

18. Moreover, recent Kyrgyz-Uzbek clashes in the Osh region of Kyrgyzstan could resume and ethnic Tadjiks in Uzbekistan may again rebel. The Uzbek minority in southern Kazakhstan is also potentially explosive. Here the primacy of ethnicity over Islamic solidarity is in clear evidence.

19. *Report by the Emergency Humanitarian Assessment Team in the New Independent States*, p. 1. In Estonia, for example, requirements for becoming a naturalized citizen prevented almost all Russian residents (an estimated one-third of the population) from participating in the country's first presidential and parliamentary elections. See Celestine Bohlen, "Estonia Rattles Its Russian Residents with Its Insistence on 'Estonization,'" *New York Times*, August 10, 1992, p. A9; and Steven Erlanger, "In the Baltics, There May Be No Home for Russians," *New York Times*, November 22, 1992, p. 1.

Union, would be regarded as internally displaced and not as refugees. She discussed the extent to which sovereignty could be used to obscure state responsibility and stressed the need for the international community to stipulate standards that would specify the obligations of sovereignty. Finally, she favored establishing a mechanism to deal with the internally displaced and advocated international action under certain conditions of a state's failure to meet its obligations toward its displaced masses.

The chairman of the Subcommittee for Refugee Affairs in the Supreme Soviet of the Russian Federation reviewed in depth the history of displacement and forced migration in the former Soviet Union. Although there had been no serious conflicts in the USSR before 1987, he explained, latent hostilities were deeply rooted in the dominant nationality's discrimination against minority nationalities. Particularly responsible for ethnic tensions was the shortsightedness of the national leadership, whose prewar repressions and deportation of masses outside their ethnic homelands planted the seeds of animosity and hatred. The problem was compounded when the USSR was partitioned into republics and people segregated among those republics. The resulting problems affected not only the Russians, but also the Georgians and the people of the central Asian republics and the Baltic states. While acknowledging the divisiveness of religious diversity, he saw religion more as something factional leaders exploited for political gain rather than as a primary cause of ethnic conflicts.

Contributing to the problems, he argued, was some politicians' exploitation of the relaxation of totalitarianism in the 1980s to exploit ethnic nationalism and conflicts to increase their political influence. Western miscalculations in encouraging Mikhail Gorbachev to allow the disintegration of the Soviet Union aggravated the nascent conflicts. The West had hoped to weaken the Soviet Union as a means of ending the cold war, but now, instead of the two superpowers quarreling, other groups have emerged that may not be easy to contain. And some of them possess nuclear weapons.

A related dangerous development, the chairman intimated, is that Russian pride has been severely hurt by the breakdown of the USSR. Russians outside Russia regard themselves as citizens of the Soviet empire, and their nationalism is now being exploited by leaders who appeal to their emotions about building an ethnically based Russian nation by advocating such policies as enforcing the use of the Russian language throughout the federation.

Focusing on the problems of the Russian minorities in the other republics, the chairman urged the international community to impress upon the leaders of those republics that although their sovereignty is recognized and respected, it cannot be allowed to compromise the human rights of the minorities. Mistreating the Russians might force them to return to Russia and become part of a political movement that could endanger the peace and stability not only of the region but of the entire world. The new states, he believed, must be pressured to protect their minorities because mistreating them could endanger the democratic process. In other words, an ethnically based nationalism that would encourage Russians to return home could result in a Russia nationalistically aggressive against the other states in the region and create a threat to regional and ultimately international peace and security.

The authorities from the Ministry of the Interior also reviewed the historical background and contemporary developments and the legislative and administrative efforts of the government to assist the displaced and the refugees. They highlighted the important role of the UN High Commissioner for Refugees in assisting refugees and displaced persons in this regard. Although the function of the Interior Ministry was presented as primarily ensuring civil order and security, the authorities showed considerable interest in international arrangements for the protection and assistance of displaced persons and refugees, treating them as equally needy. Indeed, the migrants were sometimes described as internally displaced because they acquire Russian nationality and sometimes as refugees because they come from other republics. A representative of the ministry at one point remarked that there was no problem of internally displaced persons in Russia but there was a refugee problem.

The authorities in the Ministry of Foreign Affairs welcomed the initiative of the commission in studying internal displacement. It was important, they said, for the international community to treat displacement forthrightly and to balance international responsibility and national sovereignty. "To put it crudely," one concluded, "the international community should intervene by force to protect the internally displaced where conditions make such intervention necessary." The legal and institutional manner in which the balance might be established should be openly discussed and elaborated. Although they saw a convention as the long-term objective, they favored a document of principles, a code of conduct, or a declaration with clear mechanisms for implementation as the first steps to be considered by the commission and the General Assembly.

I also held extensive discussions at the Center for Human Rights in Moscow with representatives of various groups, some of whom were spokespersons for displaced persons and refugees. Laying emphasis on protecting human rights, they argued that the government's capacity to protect ethnic Russians in the republics was limited and that international cooperation was urgently needed. They saw the problems of displaced persons and refugees as integral to the problems of the society as a whole. The solutions to those problems should therefore be sought in solutions to the problems of the society, which they considered primarily economic. To approach the problems of the displaced persons and refugees as a global crisis, which might manifest itself differently in different regions, they called for hearings or conferences at both regional and international levels.

As is apparent, Russian authorities were deeply concerned about the problems of refugees and the internally displaced, terms that they used almost interchangeably, and believed that they should be given the highest consideration, not only by the Commission on Human Rights but also by the General Assembly and the Security Council. In this respect, they were remarkably receptive to international cooperation in assisting and protecting the displaced, an attitude that contrasted sharply with the cold war attitude of the Soviet Union on such matters.

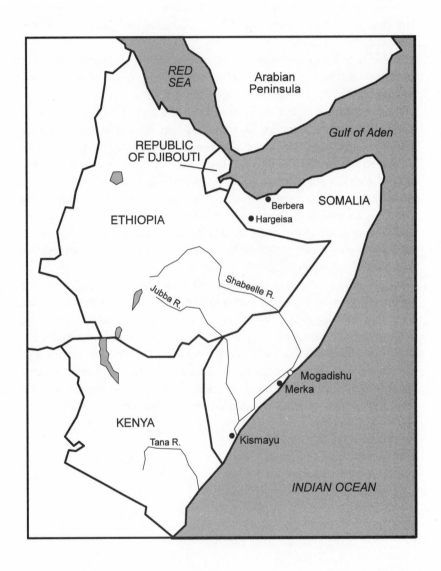

3

Somalia: From Disintegration to Reconstruction

Somalia is a humanitarian and human rights tragedy. Amnesty International has estimated that by the end of 1991 the factions representing the various Hawiye subclans based in Mogadishu had been responsible for "widespread destruction, looting and killings of unarmed civilians that left 5,000 dead and 15,000 wounded in the capital city."[1] A recent Africa Watch report has estimated that in 1992 at least 41,000 more people were killed or wounded. The report also stated that although a 1989-90 famine in south-central Somalia caused hunger and hardship for rural populations, particularly those residing in the fertile region between the Juba and Shebeele rivers, factional conflict between the United Somali Congress, the Somali Patriotic Movement, and the remnants of former President Mohamed Siad Barre's forces invading from northern Kenya had far more deadly effects: "many crops and seeds were stolen, villages destroyed and people displaced. Irrigation pumps were a particular target for looters, and fuel was often unavailable for those that remained. Tractors were also looted and people were forced to consume their harvests before their time, depleting all food reserves in the process."[2] In

---

1. Amnesty International, *Amnesty International Annual Report, 1992* (London, 1992).
2. Africa Watch, *Somalia: No Mercy in Mogadishu* (Washington: Human Rights Watch, 1992).

total an estimated 300,000 Somalis have died as a result of the war-induced famine since President Barre's overthrow in January 1991.[3]

A report prepared by the International Committee for the Red Cross emphasized that the displaced people of the country are most at risk. Among the long-term displaced, 72 percent of the children were malnourished; among the recently displaced the rate was as high as 94 percent.[4] Some observers estimate that more than 50 percent of Somalia's people are displaced. The human face of this calamity, however, is more impressively expressed in the simple words of a Somali woman: "We had 30 camels, 50 goats, 20 cows, and a house," she said. "Siad Barre's troops came. They burned the house, they took the animals, they killed my husband, and my child and I went hungry."[5]

Somalia's unrelenting chaos and misery led the United Nations to adopt a series of humanitarian actions, culminating in Security Council resolution 794 of December 3, 1992, authorizing military intervention to bring emergency assistance and help reestablish order in the country. The resolution's authorization for the international community to become actively involved in the internal affairs of a country in the name of humanitarian concern is striking. In the preamble the Security Council, "deeply disturbed by the magnitude of the human suffering" and "alarmed by the deterioration of the humanitarian situation in Somalia and underlining the urgent need for the quick delivery of humanitarian assistance in the whole country," determined that the situation constituted a threat to international peace and security in the area. In particular, the council expressed "grave alarm at continuing reports of widespread violations of international humanitarian law . . . including reports of violence and threats of violence against personnel participating lawfully in impartial humanitarian relief activities; deliberate attacks on non-combatants, relief consignments and vehicles, and medical and relief facilities; and impeding the delivery of food and medical supplies essential for the survival of the civilian population." The council also cited "reports of looting of relief supplies destined for starving people,

3. Marc Michaelson, "Somalia: The Painful Road to Reconciliation," *Africa Today*, vol. 40, no. 2 (1993), p. 53.

4. International Committee for the Red Cross, *Emergency Plan of Action: Somalia 1992*.

5. Andrew Cohen, "Humane Intervention Is Hell," *Village Voice*, January 19, 1993, p. 26.

attacks on aircraft bringing in humanitarian relief supplies, and attacks on the Pakistani UNOSOM [UN Observer Mission in Somalia] contingent in Mogadishu." It expressed determination "to establish as soon as possible the necessary conditions on the delivery of humanitarian assistance wherever needed" and "to restore peace, stability and law and order with a view to facilitating the process of a political settlement under the auspices of the United Nations, aimed at national reconciliation."

The council demanded that all factions cease hostilities immediately, maintain a cease-fire throughout the country, cooperate with UN specialized agencies and humanitarian organizations to provide assistance to the affected population, and cooperate with the secretary-general's special representative on Somalia to promote reconciliation and political settlement. The council endorsed the secretary-general's recommendation that action under chapter VII of the UN Charter should be taken as soon as possible to establish a safe environment for providing humanitarian relief. To begin the practical aspects of the operation, the council sanctioned U.S. intervention and welcomed the offers by member states to secure the relief operations.

In view of Africa's general opposition to outside intervention, it is particularly noteworthy that the African Group at the United Nations fully endorsed the request by the secretary-general.[6] The group also commended the United States for its offer to place at the disposal of the United Nations a substantial ground force and expressed the hope that nations unable to contribute troops would render logistical assistance to help make the operation a success. The African Group justified its support for the international action on humanitarian grounds: the operation was the world's response to a tragedy that had to end.

Background

Somali society has historically been shaped by the interplay of pastoral nomadism, migratory movements, coastal urbanization, and Islam.[7] For centuries before the colonial period, particularly in the hinterland where an estimated 80 percent of the population resided, clan-based political

6. *African Group on Somalia Resolution*, NY/OAU/AG/1/92 (United Nations, 1992).
7. David D. Laitin and Said S. Samatar, *Somalia: Nation in Search of a State* (Boulder, Colo.: Westview Press, 1987), pp. 1, 155.

systems practiced what I. M. Lewis termed "pastoral democracy." Pastoral and agropastoral seasonal migrations between the central plateau and the coastal plains necessitated loose cultural groupings that were at once bound by close kinship and cultural solidarity and opposed to each other by antagonistic clan interests.[8] In the tenth century, Islamic city-states developed along the Somali coast as Arab and Persian settlers brought commercial links to the larger Muslim world. These trading centers facilitated the Islamization of the country and eventually developed sophisticated administrative and legal systems based on Islamic law. Clan families became organized around various patriarchal Muslim saints.[9] By the thirteenth century the relative affluence of the coastal Muslims led to greater migration into the interior as lucrative trade routes to Abyssinia in the west were established. Increasingly, city traditions merged with the traditions of the hinterland.[10] In what was to become a recurring pattern in Somali history, interaction with other cultures encouraged a reorganization of the nation's society and politics.

In the sixteenth century, invasions from Christian Abyssinia disrupted Somali society, destroying any semblance of centralized authority. Significantly, however, instead of resorting to the anarchic warlordism that has characterized the past decade, clan leaders sought recourse in traditional law known as the Heer. A type of social contract or unwritten constitution, the Heer system transcended blood and lineage ties and, informed by traditional Islamic teachings, laid a foundation upon which social conflicts ranging from property disputes to social transactions could be resolved. The Heer was able to transcend kinship ties based solely on blood by grouping together six clans, three related by blood kinship and three smaller outside clans. In addition to establishing a delicate and complex web of negotiated agreements, the Heer stipulated that the leader (*sultan*) of the ad hoc deliberative assemblies (*shirs*) that formed

---

8. During the rainy season the lush vegetation of the central plateau and the mountainous region of the northeast attracts the herds (camels, cattle, goats, and sheep) of the Somali nomads. In the dry season they are forced to migrate to a string of wells along the coast.

9. The major branches of the Somali lineage system were thus based on the pastoral clans of the Dir, Darod, Isaak, and Hawiye and the agricultural clans of the Digil and Rahanwayn in the more fertile regions in southern Somalia.

10. This merger between the coastal and hinterland traditions was clear by the sixteenth century when the Muslim state of Adal was born. Adal was the leading state in a Muslim confederation extending from northern Ethiopia into northern Somalia and what is now Djibouti until its invasion and defeat in 1542 by the Christian Abyssinian kingdom.

the functional basis of the Heer had to be chosen from one of the outside clans to balance the power of the dominant clans and families.[11]

Clearly then, although Somalia has long been considered one of the few homogeneous countries in Africa, homogeneity is a relative concept. The Somali social system is actually one that anthropologists term *acephalous*, a segmentary lineage system in which social order is maintained by balancing opposing segments on the same social level, clans and tribes against each other and lineages, families, and individuals against other lineages, families, and individuals. Although members of a family, lineage, clan, or tribe may unite against an external threat, the unity is often undermined by internal rivalry and the need for external alliances. It is the balance the Heer was meant to maintain, and it is the balance that was disrupted first by the colonial powers and later by Siad Barre who sought to destroy it after Somalia gained independence.

In the nineteenth century what many Somali nationalists term Greater Somalia became the focus of intense colonial competition that partitioned the territory among British Somaliland in the north, Italian Somaliland in the south, and French Somaliland (present-day Djibouti) in the northwest. The territory of the Ogaden in the west was occupied by imperial Ethiopia. The hitherto resilient Heer system was altered, albeit not transformed, as arbitrary force came to determine the relationship between increasingly centralized colonial states and increasingly fragmented Somali communities with competing political and economic interests determined by their respective historical experiences. Somali scholar Abdi Samatar has argued that it was this development "rather than Somali society or traditions which represents the genesis of contemporary Somali dictatorship and warlordism."[12]

The British and Italian colonial traditions left distinctly different imprints in northern and southern Somalia. Considerable variations in education, legal systems, tariffs, customs dues, and patterns of trade distinguished the British administration from that established by the Italians.[13] The British demonstrated little interest in developing Somalia and were content to confine their administration to the coastal areas.

11. See Laitan and Samatar, *Somalia: Nation in Search of a State*, pp. 41–44.

12. Abdi Samatar, "Dictators and Warlords Are a Modern Invention," *Africa News*, December 21, 1992—January 3, 1993, p. 5.

13. I. M. Lewis, *A Modern History of Somalia: Nation and State in the Horn of Africa*, (Boulder, Colo.: Westview Press, 1987), pp. 170–71.

The Italians hoped to garner some economic benefit from their colony. Between 1920 and 1940 Italy introduced large-scale plantation farming in the interriverine areas of the south and established more advanced educational and health services, which largely explains the domination of jobs and other privileges by southern bureaucrats following independence. In addition, the colonial partition of Somalia cut off many dominant pastoral families from their traditional grazing lands and migratory routes, disrupting their social cohesiveness. The goal of reuniting the Somali people into a Greater Somalia that preoccupied many Somali nationalists and eventually led to hostilities with Somalia's neighbors was in part motivated by the desire to reestablish direct control over grazing areas that were vital to the economies of the various clans.

When Italian Somaliland and British Somaliland received their independence in 1960 and united to form the Somali Republic, the foreign experts who hastily drafted the transitional constitution paid little attention to reviving social institutions such as the Heer that might have been able to channel resilient clan loyalties and parochial interests into achieving national objectives.[14] For their part the aspiring Somali nationalists, in the fashion of postindependence elites elsewhere, were so consumed with the independence struggle that they failed to examine their new state's internal differences or decide on the distribution of political power and economic resources.

The regime that came into being after the unification of the territories reflected this failure to plan. From its outset the distribution of government power was biased in favor of the South. The offices of president and prime minister, most cabinet posts, and the most important positions in the military and police were awarded to southern Somalis, which caused increasing resentment among the northerners. The incompetence and corruption of the postcolonial parliamentary period, encouraged by the degeneration of political parties into factions with clan and subclan affiliations, brought about the downfall of the Western-style democracy in 1969. When southerner Mohamed Siad Barre seized power

14. Hussein M. Adam, "Rethinking the Somali Political Experience," paper presented at the U.S. Institute of Peace Public Workshop on Political Reconciliation and Reconstruction in Somalia, Washington, October 16, 1992. See similar arguments by Adam in "Somalia: Militarism, Warlordism or Democracy?" *Review of African Political Economy*, no. 54 (July 1992), pp. 11-26.

in a coup, the Somali's desire for peace and stability was so strong that he received a hero's welcome.

The welcome soon grew thin. Following his 1978 defeat by Ethiopia in a conflict over which country would control the Ogaden region, opposition to Barre's regime expanded.[15] Barre had neither the foresight nor the aptitude to design a more representative system. Instead, he concentrated power further into his own hands, so much so that although he initially included members of his Darod clan in his cabinet, by the end of the regime in 1991 he could trust only members of his immediate family.

This concentration of power depended on two intertwined strategies, the repression of internal opposition and the courtship of outside support. To control internal dissention, Barre turned to external alliances, and in this the politics of the cold war was pivotal. He became a master at playing the superpowers against one another, transferring loyalty from East to West, amassing arms from both, inciting a war with Ethiopia, keeping Kenya under constant apprehension by reviving the Somali's historical claim over the latter's Northern Frontier District (of which an estimated half of the population is ethnic Somali) in his drive for a Greater Somalia, and maintaining a firm grip on internal unrest.

These polices accounted for his durability. But well before the collapse of the Soviet Union the support from the superpowers dwindled and the internal threat to his power grew stronger. Increasingly he depended on violent repression and the tactics of pitting clans against clans, families against families. In an exhaustive analysis of his record published in 1990, Africa Watch declared that "for nearly a decade before any armed insurgencies, the army and the security forces, immune from prosecution, sought to stamp out dissent and prohibit criticism of government by extreme systematic oppression." The report confirmed that Barre's aerial bombardment of the insurrectionary Isaak clan in northern Somalia killed 50,000 to 60,000 noncombatants between May 1988 and January 1990 and caused the displacement of as many as 800,000 people, half of whom fled to refugee camps in Ethiopia.[16]

15. Somalis have long insisted that the Ogaden region is part of western Somalia, claiming it was seized by Emperor Menelik of Ethiopia in the late nineteenth century.

16. Africa Watch, *Somalia: A Government at War with Its Own People* (Washington: Human Rights Watch, 1990).

Setting the pattern of the crisis to come, Barre began to arm clans against his Isaak enemies, most notably the Ogadeni refugees who had been displaced following the 1977–78 war with Ethiopia. Moreover, according to I. M. Lewis, "Ogadeni refugees [were] encouraged to take over the remains of Isaak shops and houses. Thus, those who were received as refugee guests . . . supplanted their Isaak hosts, many of whom in this bitterly ironic turn of fate are now refugees in the Ogaden."[17] In addition, Barre carefully cultivated and received the support of the non-Isaak clans in the North—the Gadabursi, Dulbhante, and Warsangeli—who traditionally competed with their Isaak neighbors over grazing land and water resources and now took up arms with Barre's troops against them. Beginning in 1989 he pursued this same policy of favoritism when the clans of southern and central Somalia started to support the two rebel movements in the region, the Somali Patriotic Movement (SPM) and the United Somali Congress (USC).

In response to growing human rights violations, a group from the Isaak clan, arguably the most aggrieved of Barre's enemies, formed the Somali National Movement (SNM) in 1981 and from across the border in Ethiopia began engaging in military operations against Barre's army. On May 31, 1988, the SNM attacked the northern city of Hargeisa, which resulted in bloody reprisals by the Somali army that left tens of thousands of innocent civilians dead throughout the North. A year later the guerrilla warfare spread to the central and southern parts of the country as the Hawiye and the Ogaden clans rebelled, coordinating their strategy with the SNM in the North.

By the time Barre's regime finally fell, several rebel groups had gained effective control of various regions of the country. Somalia, as a unified nation, ceased to exist as leaders of many factions asserted clan identities in their struggle to gain control over as big a patch of territory as possible. In the North the Somali National Movement dominated. The Somali Salvation Democratic Front (SSDF), consisting mainly of the Majerteen, a subclan of Barre's own Darod clan, was active in the northeast and central regions. Formed in 1978, this was the oldest opposition force, albeit it has had comparatively little military success. In the South the Somali Patriotic Movement was made up of Ogadeni,

---

17. I. M. Lewis, "The Ogaden and the Fragility of Somali Segmented Nationalism," *Horn of Africa*, vol. 13 (January–March 1990), p. 59

another subclan of the Darod. Between the Juba and Shebeele rivers in the southwest the Rahanwein were represented by the Somali Democratic Movement whose weak social position reflects their mixture of nomadism and dry-land farming. Possessing the most fertile region in the country, the Rahanwein were the main victims of the famine and violence as powerful neighboring warlords sought to displace them. In the center, and around the capital of Mogadishu, now all but destroyed, was the Hawiye-based United Somali Congress. The USC, founded one year before Barre's ouster, was a relative newcomer to the conflict, but came to occupy a prominent position in 1990. When the party broke up the following year into the Hawiye subclans of the Haber Gidir led by Ali Mahdi and the Abgal led by Mohamed Farah Aideed, even before Aideed finally drove Barre from Somalia into Kenya, internecine violence increased dramatically, as did the number of deaths and displaced persons in the South.[18] The fateful decision of southerner Ali Mahdi to declare himself president in a hastily convened 1991 "reconciliation" conference in Djibouti within days after Aideed's forces had driven Barre out of Mogadishu caused an escalation of the violence in and around the capital. Aideed refused to recognize Mahdi's appointment and attacked his forces in Mogadishu while the largest clan in the North, the Isaaks, grew increasingly apprehensive and broke off their precarious alliance with the southern-based USC and SPM. Years of northerner's resentment culminated in their unilateral declaration of an independent Republic of Somaliland in May 1991.

It is within this context, and with over a million people starving to death, that the UN Security Council and the U.S. Congress passed resolutions in July 1992 condemning the factional violence and preparing the ground for the humanitarian intervention five months later.

Observations

The first evidence of the breakdown of civil order to meet a new arrival in Mogadishu during the peak of the crisis was the sight of the technicals, vehicles carrying young men armed with automatic weapons

18. Africa Watch, *Somalia: A Fight to the Death?* (Washington: Human Rights Watch, February 13, 1992), p. 3.

that they brandished with obvious relish, often flashing smiles.[19] All over the war-ravaged city, its whitewashed walls pocked with bullet holes, the struggle for survival revealed itself in the seemingly flourishing trade in local commodities and crowds of displaced persons clustering inside abandoned houses. But no significant activity, and in particular no movement, seemed possible without the protection of the armed guards in their technicals.

Despite the anarchy in Mogadishu, supplies were available, and the displaced were in far better condition than they were in the rest of Somalia. But logistics prevented me from traveling to the worst areas within the short time available. In addition, the growing danger of violence made the UN Observer Mission in Somalia close off the northern part of Mogadishu itself, so that apart from the UN officials, I was able to meet only with General Aideed, the factional leader with the largest part of the city under his control. Ali Mahdi, who was considered more cooperative by the international community, controlled the part that UNOSOM had closed off, presumably to prevent attacks by Aideed's forces.

In my meeting with them, Aideed and his aides seemed optimistic that the war would end soon, clearly seeing their faction as the winner. Thinking beyond the fighting and responding to the humanitarian challenges of the situation, they urged assistance to the internally displaced to enable them to resume a self-sustaining life. The immediate challenge, they said, was to save lives by providing food, shelter, and other essential needs. The people should then be settled in agriculturally productive lands where they should be provided with social services and means of production—education, health facilities, water supply, housing, agricultural tools, and for the coastal people, fishing materials.

Aideed and his aides also contributed ideas for reconstructing Somali society that may still prove practical and, in fact, not too different from what was being done through the skillful management of Ambassador Robert Oakley, the special U.S. envoy to Somalia. The international community, they argued, should channel assistance through local authorities—clan elders—identified and approved by the leaders of the dominant movements in the respective areas. In this manner, future

19. The term supposedly originated from a ploy by the regional director of UNICEF who, forbidden by the UN regulations from employing armed guards, justified hiring them as "technical services."

district and regional authorities could acquire legitimacy and become effective in restoring order. They suggested that the old judicial system at the district and the regional levels be reactivated. Experts, including Somalis themselves, saw the elders as a valuable resource in reconstructing society and the state. It is worth noting in this regard that some observers have identified peace initiatives reminiscent of efforts in the Heer tradition in the central and northern parts of the country.[20] These efforts may provide the best basis for social reconstruction managed by the United States and the international community.

The factional Somali leaders were strongly divided on the extent that external intervention would be beneficial. Ali Mahdi accepted the participation of the United Nations, presumably because his status as appointed president, while of no practical consequence, gave him some semblance of international legitimacy. But General Aideed, the most militarily powerful of the competing leaders, was in my meeting with him uncompromising in his opposition to international intervention. The fact that he subsequently accepted UN forces can only be explained by pragmatism and self-interest in acknowledging the fait accompli of Operation Restore Hope. In an acutely divided country, there will always be elements favoring and elements opposed to intervention from outside, and positions will often change with the dynamics of the situation.[21]

By the summer of 1993, perhaps because disarming the militias compromised the superiority of his military position, Aideed believed that the presence of UN forces tipped the political balance in favor of Ali Mahdi. He repeatedly accused the foreign troops of interfering in Somalia's political affairs and undermining his own efforts to make peace among various Somali factions in the spirit of agreements signed in Addis Ababa earlier in the year.[22] Relations between Aideed and the UN troops

20. Rakiya Omaar and Alex de Waal have emphasized that a "delicate web of negotiated agreements" has allowed for the return of some semblance of stability in some areas. See "Somalia's Uninvited Saviours: The West May Be Stepping on People It Wants to Help," *Washington Post*, December 13, 1992, p. C4; and "Saving Somalia without the Somalis," *Africa News*, December 21, 1992–January 3, 1993, p. 4.

21. For a detailed account of the various factional leaders' ties and attitudes with respect to external intervention, see "Somalia: Warlords Meet the New World Order," *Africa Confidential*, December 4, 1992, pp. 1–3.

22. "Gunmen, UN Troops Exchange Fire in Mogadishu," Agence France Presse, June 5, 1993, in Foreign Broadcast Information Service, *Daily Report: Sub-Saharan Africa*, June 7, 1993, p. 4; and Mogadishu Radio Mogadishu, "Aidid Accuses U.S. of Complicity, Warns UNOSOM," June 5, 1993, in FBIS: *Daily Report: Sub-Saharan Africa*, June 7, 1993, p. 5.

continued to deteriorate, and on June 5 Aideed loyalists ambushed and killed twenty-four Pakistani UN soldiers who, following their mandate, were confiscating weapons in an area of Mogadishu under Aideed's control. Less than two weeks later UN peacekeeping forces led by U.S. troops launched retaliatory air strikes, designed to destroy Aideed's power base in southwestern Mogadishu, that caused heavy civilian casualties. Apprehensive over Aideed's superior weaponry and resentful of his unwillingness to abide by a March 1993 disarmament agreement that conceded the supervision of the disarmament to the United Nations, rival factions, most notably that of Ali Mahdi, which controlled northern Mogadishu, publicly commended the UN troops for taking the "right action" against Aideed.

However, the UN and U.S. strategy of undermining Aideed's strength and thereby gaining the support of other factional leaders and the Somali people is far from certain given the country's history with external intervention and the fluidity with which clan networks are aligned and severed.[23] Meanwhile, violence has resulted in a mounting toll of civilian deaths and casualties. According to the International Committee of the Red Cross, one UN raid alone killed at least 54 Somalis and injured 174 others.[24] Security in many parts of Mogadishu has deteriorated so much that the delivery of relief supplies has been dramatically slowed, which has set off criticism of the UN operation.[25] All in all, it would seem that the transition from the first phase of Operation Restore Hope, which the Somalis welcomed, to the longer-term UN mission of restoring and consolidating civil order, which the Somalis see as turning foreign troops into an army of occupation, has created complications for the international community that will not be easy to resolve.

23. The *Financial Times* reports that after several incidents in which UN soldiers fired into crowds, and many U.S.-dropped bombs, the Somalis in Mogadishu resent the foreign presence and are rallying around General Aideed instead of the UN's peacekeeping efforts. See Leslie Crawford, "Somalis Condemn UN Air Raids," *Financial Times*, June 15, 1993, p. 1.

24. See Keith B. Richburg, "Reality in Mogadishu: A Conflict in Views," *Washington Post*, July 14, 1993, p. A18.

25. Italy has reportedly called for a halt to military action and negotiations with Aideed, while the Organization of African Unity has urged UN restraint and dialogue with Aideed. However, Madeleine Albright, the U.S. Ambassador to the United Nations, who visited Somalia in early July, admonished journalists for negative reports, insisting that the "real Somalis" support the UN effort. See Richburg, "Reality in Mogadishu," p. A18.

The fundamental challenge of the Somali situation is, then, for the various forces not only to address the mass starvation and displacement but to consider the causes of the crisis, the breakdown of civil order and the factors behind the breakdown. Restructuring society and restoring a self-sustaining social order are ultimately the only solutions to the Somali crisis. Once protection and assistance are achieved, UN efforts will have to focus on reconstructing civil society with institutions and guarantees that protect human rights.

Reconstruction will have to involve a more democratic government, one that will become the basis for unity among the peoples of Somalia. This should not, however, mean that the values and institutions of the clan system will become irrelevant. Quite the contrary, a political, economic, and social system that values local resources and resourcefulness can be designed to reconcile the lofty ideals of unity with the reality of segmentation and fragmentation in Somali society. The institutions of the family, the clan, and the tribe can indeed be complementary rather than antagonistic to the nation.

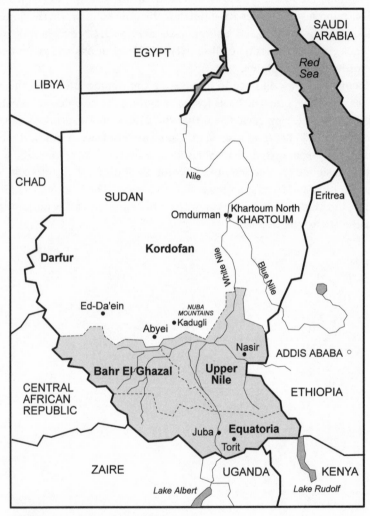

SOUTHERN PROVINCES

4

The Sudan:
A Nation Divided

My visit to the Sudan was more complex than the visits to the other countries, partly because I am a Sudanese national who has held official positions in the country and been intimately involved in the search for peace. Given this background and considering that the Sudan is one of the countries in which war-generated displacement is most acute, I was aware of the precariousness of my role, which raised the question of whether I should exclude the country from the list of those I was to visit. I chose to visit it, however, although my mission there would be inherently more difficult than would be the case elsewhere.

Even more than I had expected, the program organized for me was, in comparison to those in the other countries, extensive, intensive, and indeed, challenging to me in addressing the problems of internal displacement. This depth accounts for the relative length of this chapter and the detailed analysis of the situation.

Background

The drought of 1983–85 in the western and eastern Sudan and the subsequent famine cost many lives and triggered massive dislocations of people in those regions. Although the government was reluctant to invite international relief operations, diplomatic pressures eventually succeeded in getting it to change its position, and an unprecedented international emergency operation arrested the crisis. But most of the displacement problems of the Sudan have resulted from a civil war that has raged since 1983 between successive governments and the southern-

65

based Sudan People's Liberation Movement and its army (SPLM-SPLA). Some 5 million southern Sudanese have been uprooted, and 500,000 have been forced to seek refuge in neighboring countries. Most initially went to Ethiopia, but following the overthrow of the government of Colonel Mengistu Haile Mariam in May 1990, they moved to other countries in east Africa, in particular Kenya and Uganda. Perhaps 3 million have moved to northern rural areas or to urban centers where they live in appalling conditions as squatters. Most of the displaced remain in the South, enduring the hardships of life in a war zone.

Although the first great wave of displaced persons arrived in Khartoum from the Arabized and Islamized western regions of Kordofan and Darfur in 1984 as a result of the drought, by the late 1980s the greatest number were members of southern pastoral ethnic groups—Dinka, Shilluk, Nuer—from the districts of Bahr el-Ghazal and Upper Nile who were fleeing the increasingly brutal war in the South. Their influx coincided with a deliberate government policy of heavily arming Arab and even non-Arab tribes in the border regions so as to weaken the Dinka-dominated SPLA. Africa Watch has reported that tribal militia, in a thinly disguised counterinsurgency campaign promoted by the "democratically elected" government of the time, had by the late 1980s massacred hundreds of civilians.[1] This campaign, in combination with a famine of unprecedented severity, devastated the South. Africa Watch has estimated that since 1986, some 500,000 civilians have died as a result of war and famine. Although the objectives of both the government and the SPLA were ostensibly war-related, the tribal militias charged with perpetrating atrocities were motivated by long-held hostilities and the chance to loot livestock and expropriate additional pastoral lands by forcing out indigenous groups.

With religious tensions aggravating intertribal hostilities, the brutalities of the Arab-Muslim militia against the *kufar* (the infidels, or southern animists) increased. There are gruesome eyewitness accounts of pregnant women cut open and living fetuses extracted, of men slaughtered by having their throats cut, and of children and women carried off to be held for ransom or sold into slavery. Two Khartoum University lecturers have documented the slave trade and the massacre of more than a

---

1. Africa Watch, *Denying "the Honor of Living": Sudan, a Human Rights Disaster* (Washington: Human Rights Watch, 1990).

thousand displaced Dinka men, women, and children in the western town of Dhien on March 27–28, 1987.[2] The scholars were condemned, harassed, and even threatened with prosecution by the government. The prime minister accused them of libel against the Muslim Missiriyya tribe, arguing that what the tribesmen had been engaged in was not slavery in the classic sense but a customary practice of intertribal warfare.

Three years after the international relief operations that alleviated the famine in the North, the conflict in the South had caused unprecedented numbers of deaths from starvation. In their pursuit of the civil war, successive governments and the rebels both used food as a primary weapon, obstructing relief supplies, denying famine-stricken populations freedom of movement and residence and, in some cases, executing relief workers. In 1988 alone an estimated 250,000 people, almost all of them civilians, lost their lives in the conflict-related famine. The international community responded in 1989 by launching a second massive assistance program, Operation Lifeline Sudan, involving governments and nongovernmental organizations coordinated by the United Nations. The program was widely credited with averting a repetition of the 1988 tragedy. Lifeline has been renegotiated several times and has been acclaimed as a model of success in humanitarianism, one that has been emulated in other crisis situations.[3] But the starving masses of southern Sudanese continue to be victims of the civil war. It is a human rights calamity that is increasingly affecting the entire country.

Although modern Sudanese history has been characterized by human rights violations in the South, both the war and the violations have intensified under the military government of Lieutenant General Omar al-Bashir, which seized power on June 30, 1989. To appreciate how crucial the human rights record of the Sudan has become in the country's international relations, one must understand developments since the coup and the responses from the international community. The

2. Ushari Ahmed Mahmud and Suleyman Ali Baldo, *The Dhien Massacre: Slavery in the Sudan* (London: Sudan Relief and Rehabilitation Association, 1987). The book is also an account of the practice of slavery by the Arab tribes of western Sudan. A prominent religious leader intimated to me that he and other leaders were receiving letters from their Arab followers inquiring whether it was ordained or forbidden by Islam to kill a Dinka. Burning the villages, destroying the crops, and looting livestock were among the methods used by the Arab militia to decimate Dinka sources of livelihood.

3. See Francis M. Deng and Larry Minear, *The Challenges of Famine Relief: Emergency Operations in the Sudan* (Brookings, 1992).

regime immediately suspended the national constitution, dissolved all political parties, trade unions, and civil associations, and repealed freedoms of the press, assembly, movement, and residence. In addition, a report by Amnesty International in 1992 stated that the government has engaged in "routine torture and ill-treatment" of Sudanese citizens. Detentions and extrajudicial killings have become commonplace not only in Khartoum but also in the Nuba mountains of western Sudan and in Darfur in the far west.[4]

The most egregious human rights violations, however, continue to occur in the South. International observers have consistently accused the government of brutalities against civilians it suspects of being sympathetic to the Sudan People's Liberation Army. According to both Amnesty International and Africa Watch, the rebels, though to a lesser extent, have also been responsible for human rights violations against noncombatants, engaging in extrajudicial executions, including the killing of captured soldiers and suspected political dissidents.[5]

The regime is widely reported to pursue a policy inherited from the previous government of forcibly relocating massive numbers of people from the capital to inhospitable desert camps. In 1992 Africa Watch reported that the government had "bulldozed and burned the homes of about 500,000 of its poorest citizens in a forcible and violent program of expulsions from Khartoum . . . in violation of fundamental legal principles, such as barring legal actions on behalf of the squatters, and in abrogation of established Sudanese land tenure practices." In one instance camp residents were said to have been killed by government forces while attempting to protest forced relocation. According to the same report, at least 100,000 of the 500,000 relocated so far have been moved to an extremely arid plain known ironically as Dar-es-Salaam, "Haven of Peace," west of Omdurman, which reportedly lacks even the most basic shelter, water supplies, and sanitation.[6]

Southerners and foreign observers believe the relocation program is part of a strategy of religious and ethnic purification. A study commissioned by the U.S. Committee for Refugees in 1990 claimed that northerners considered the "large number of displaced southerners in

4. Amnesty International, *Sudan: A Continuing Human Rights Crisis* (London, 1992).
5. Amnesty International, *Sudan*; and Africa Watch, *Denying "the Honor of Living."*
6. Africa Watch, *Sudan: Refugees in Their Own Country* (Washington: Human Rights Watch, 1992).

Khartoum [to] constitute a security threat. Furthermore, representatives of pro-Islamic political groups hold the view that refugees, most of whom are non-Muslim, dilute the 'religious purity' of Khartoum and other northern regions."[7] A campaign against the Muslim but non-Arab Nuba of southern Kordofan, many of whom have joined the SPLM-SPLA, has been termed ethnic cleansing. The government has reportedly embarked on an attempt to eliminate the Nuba as part of the war against the SPLA.[8] In 1992 Africa Watch claimed that extrajudicial arrests and executions of the Nuba as well as massive relocations to regions further north implied an initiative to eradicate their culture in the name of achieving a more "orthodox" Islamic identity.[9] Six camps near the regional capital of Kadugli are said to contain 25,000 displaced people, and many Nuba have allegedly been forcibly trucked to northern Kordofan.

The government flatly and bitterly disputes these allegations. There can, however, be no question about the brutality of the civil war, the racial, ethnic, religious, and cultural divisions that caused it and that have in turn been aggravated by it, and the alienation of the southern people who view any faction that assumes power in the North as "colonial" and lacking legitimacy.

Because of the military coup, the intensification of the civil war in the South, and the mounting allegations of human rights violations, the international community and the United Nations have become concerned. The analytical report of the secretary-general on internally displaced persons summarized some of the pertinent findings of nongovernmental organizations and referred to the alleged use of violence to force internally displaced people from the South and the West out of Khartoum in 1987 during the period of parliamentary democracy.[10]

7. U.S. Committee for Refugees, *Khartoum's Displaced Persons: A Decade of Despair* (Washington, 1990).

8. On December 9, 1992, the British House of Lords condemned what was described as ethnic cleansing of the black African population by the Islamic fundamentalist military regime in Khartoum. For further discussion on the debate in the British Parliament, see Colin Legum, "Horn of Africa: Rising International Concern over Sudan," *Third World Reports* (January 13, 1993), pp. 1–13; and Bona Malwal, "British Lords Condemn Ethnic Cleansing in Sudan," *Sudan Democratic Gazette*, January 1992, p. 8.

9. Africa Watch, *Sudan: Eradicating the Nuba* (Washington: Human Rights Watch, 1992).

10. *Analytical Report of the Secretary-General on Internally Displaced Persons* (United Nations, 1992), paras. 43, 59, 66.

In 1992 the execution of southern Sudanese who worked for the U.S. Agency for International Development in Juba for alleged collaboration with the SPLM-SPLA set off a wave of Western reaction that culminated in a resolution by the U.S. Senate condemning human rights violations in the Sudan and a debate in the British House of Lords. The European Parliament also condemned the human rights situation in the Sudan.[11]

On December 12, 1992, after the under secretary-general for humanitarian affairs had visited the Sudan in an effort to intercede with the parties and facilitate the delivery of humanitarian assistance, the UN General Assembly adopted resolution 47/L.77 in which it expressed "deep concern at the serious human rights violations in the Sudan, including summary executions, detentions without due process, forced displacement of persons and torture." It urged the government "to respect fully human rights" and all parties "to cooperate in order to ensure such respect." The resolution also called on the government "to comply with applicable international instruments of human rights, in particular the International Covenants on Human Rights and the Convention on the Elimination of All Forms of Racial Discrimination, to which the Sudan is a party, and to ensure that all individuals in its territory and subject to its jurisdiction, including members of all religious and ethnic groups, enjoy the rights recognized in those instruments."[12]

The resolution asked the special rapporteur on extrajudicial, summary, or arbitrary executions "to address the killing of Sudanese national employees of foreign government relief organizations" and called on the government "to ensure a full, thorough and prompt investigation of the killings by an independent judicial inquiry commission, to bring to justice those responsible and provide just compensations to the families of the victims." The General Assembly was "alarmed by the large number of internally displaced persons and victims of discrimination in the Sudan, including members of minorities who have been forcibly displaced in violation of their human rights and who are in need of relief assistance and of protection." It called on all parties to permit international agencies, humanitarian organizations, and donor governments to

11. House of Lords, *Official Reports*, vol. 541, no. 73 (London), pp. 268–308; and "EC Condemns Juba Executions," *Sudan Update*, vol. 4 (October 19, 1992), p. 2.

12. General Assembly, *Resolution on Human Rights Situation in Sudan*, A/C.3/47/ L.77 (United Nations, December 2, 1992).

deliver humanitarian assistance and to cooperate with the UN Department of Humanitarian Affairs.

To appreciate the moral vacuum into which those fleeing, especially from the South, fall, it is essential to understand the conflict and the enmities it has created. The Sudan is certainly one of the countries in Africa most acutely divided by racial, ethnic, cultural, linguistic, and religious differences. Although there is a great deal of racial and ethnic overlap, the Arab Muslim North and the more indigenously African South, whose leadership is mostly Christian, see little in common. Geographical barriers isolated the two until the nineteenth century when their encounter began a bitter history of slave raids by the North. They were unified into one country by colonial rule but administered separately until independence, when they were lumped into a single state. Their differences are compounded by disparities in the levels of political, economic, social, and cultural development—the North being more advanced. Conflict between the two broke out in the months before independence on January 1, 1956. The fighting was halted by the military rule of President Jaafar Mohamed Nimeiri through the highly acclaimed Addis Ababa Agreement of 1972 that gave the South regional autonomy, but it resumed in 1983 when Nimeiri himself abrogated the agreement.

In September 1983 Nimeiri imposed the infamous Sharia Islamic laws, presumably to retain the loyalty of Islamic fundamentalists, the only group that then supported him. Poor southern Christians and destitute Muslims from the western Sudan became the main victims of the harsh and, most would agree, inhumane criminal penalties, which include flogging for consuming, possessing, or trading alcohol, amputation of hands for even a petty theft, and cross-amputation of hands and feet in cases of theft involving violence. Adultery, although difficult to prove in Islamic law, is punished by stoning to death. Islamics vehemently defend these penalties on both legal and moral grounds, considering them as means of purifying society from corruption and degeneration. However, the September Laws, as they came to be called, formally and perhaps irrevocably made religion the most divisive factor in the conflict and replanted the seeds of secessionist thinking among southerners.

The relationship between Islam and the state has been debated in the Sudan since independence (although Nimeiri was the first to impose Sharia by presidential decree), but the present government of Lieutenant General al-Bashir has proved to be the most unwaveringly committed to the law and the establishment of an Islamic state. Since assuming power, ostensibly to save Sharia from being revoked by an impending compromise with the rebel movement that had been popularly imposed on the prime minister, the "Revolution of National Salvation" has declared *jihad* (holy war) to mobilize the Muslim community against the SPLM-SPLA. The government has also systematically moved to implement the agenda of the National Islamic Front, the most vocal and best organized advocate for an Islamic state.[13] The ultimate objective is to establish an Islamic state in the Sudan and then spread the cause of Islamic revivalism to all of sub-Saharan and North Africa. As a result, religion, specifically the role of Sharia in public affairs, has emerged as the crucial factor in the conflict.

The government is confronted with serious challenges in the South and in the North, where leaders of banned political parties, military commanders, Muslim secularists, and other factions have combined with the SPLM-SPLA to form the National Democratic Alliance (NDA), whose objective is to overthrow the regime. The challenge confronting the government thus emanates not only from its Islamic character in a nation of religious diversity but also from its militarism and its opposition to the pluralism of party politics (the government seeks instead to legitimize itself by involving the people in decisionmaking, using both its interpretation of Islamic doctrine and its notion of consultations).

The revivalist orientation of the regime also entails potential or actual conflict between the relative and the universal standards on which international protection is founded. Relativism can be construed in two incompatible ways. It can be argued that all cultures have their distinctive ways of promoting and protecting human dignity, and in that sense relativism reinforces the universal principles of human rights rather than conflicts with them. A different interpretation would argue that relativism upholds unusual standards for human rights to justify and defend local practices that may contradict the universal standards presented in international instruments. Lashing for consuming or trading in alcohol, amputation for theft, or death by stoning for adultery are practices imposed by Islamic law that would be considered cruel and inhumane by

13. For details on the Islamic fundamentalist movement in the Sudan, see Abdelwahab El-Affendi, *Turabi's Revolution: Islam and Power in Sudan* (London: Grey Seal Books, 1990); and El-Affendi, *Who Needs an Islamic State?* (London: Grey Seal Books, 1991).

universal human rights standards. This makes conflict between relativism and universalism inevitable. The example of the Sudan shows that this conflict may indeed be deeply rooted.

A brief account of the Islamic movement in the Sudan may elucidate the point. Islamic fundamentalism sprang up in reaction both to colonialism, which promoted Christianity and Western concepts of secular nationhood, and to the collaboration of traditional Muslim leaders with foreign powers, which reinforced conservatism in the face of pressures for modernization. A twin movement, indeed the first to be born, was communism. Both were primarily pragmatic reactions to domestic conditions and used ideology only as a tool of domestic political cohesion and global outreach in an interconnected world. With the demise of communism in the Sudan after an abortive coup in 1971, which Nimeiri used as a pretext to deliver a debilitating blow to the Communist party, and then the demise internationally with the collapse of the Soviet Union and Eastern Europe, Muslim revivalists remained the only credible alternative to traditional political forces. The Muslim Brothers, who transformed themselves politically into the Islamic Charter Front and the National Islamic Front, infiltrated the army and won the support of the officers who took over on June 30, 1989.[14]

Islam in the Sudan has been closely associated with Arabism as a composite racial, cultural, and religious identity. But the challenge that faces the Muslim revivalists is how to reconcile their religious legitimacy and basis of power with the diverse value systems within the nation-state and the world. Western values and institutions, including the separation of religion and the state, that have thus far dominated the nation-state system have been adopted and internalized even by much of the Muslim community. In the South of the Sudan, national identity has evolved along indigenous African, Christian, and more Western secular lines that contrast with the Arab-Islamic model of the North. Indeed, the two appear to thrive on their mutual antagonism and struggle for survival. And because the international political culture is more favorably disposed toward secularism, the regime sees itself as confronting not only national secularists but an international secularist conspiracy.

14. For a discussion of the factors leading to the rise of Islamic fundamentalism in the Sudan, see Riad Ibrahim [Khalid Medani], "Factors Contributing to the Political Ascendancy of the Muslim Brethren in Sudan," *Arab Studies Quarterly*, vol. 12 (Summer–Fall 1990), pp. 33–53.

In my discussions with them, Sudanese authorities often argued that the standards of human rights postulated by the international community do not reflect the values or aspirations of Muslims. This, combined with the regime's determination to promote its Islamic agenda with ruthless and unwavering use of force, has placed the Sudan under international scrutiny. But the authorities perceive the attention as a campaign by the West against the Islamic orientation of the regime rather than a justified response to human rights violations.

Observations

The objective of my visit to the Sudan, as indeed of my visits to the other countries except the former Yugoslavia, where I accompanied Tadeusz Mazowiecki, the special rapporteur on the human rights conditions there, was not to monitor human rights violations but to consult with the government on my mandate with a view to ensuring official support. The attitude of the international community toward violations of rights in the Sudan was indeed a matter of grave concern to the authorities and figured prominently in my discussions with them. The draft of the General Assembly resolution was being circulated and debated during my visit.[15] This in part explains the attention that the visit received and the misperception by many that it was an investigative mission.

Because internally displaced persons were the focus of the mandate, the human rights debate during my visit focused on the forcible removal of southern squatters to the desolate areas outside Khartoum, a measure widely perceived as an effort to rid the capital of people whose behavior deviated from the norms defined by the Islamic Revolution for National Salvation. And indeed, the clash of values was rendered more acute because many of the displaced women produced alcoholic beverages as their main source of income. Confrontation with the police on this matter has been a notorious feature of their lives. Many women have been flogged or jailed and their utensils for brewing destroyed, but they have continued to violate the law for lack of alternative livelihoods.

In preparing for my visit I asked to see the two camps for the displaced near Khartoum—Dar-es-Salaam, west of Omdurman, and Jebel Awlia, south of Khartoum—and to visit other centers in Kordofan, including

15. General Assembly, *Resolution on Human Rights Situation in Sudan.*

Abyei on the North-South border, where people fleeing from the war in the South and those returning from the North converged. The government granted both requests.

In seeking the support of my mandate from the government, I used two main arguments. First, the Sudan needed to address the crisis of displacement and the implications for human rights violations. It also needed international cooperation to assist it in trying to resolve the problems. Second, given its poor international reputation on human rights matters, the country stood to gain diplomatically from facing the problems and supporting, indeed championing, the initiatives on internal displacement of the Commission on Human Rights. In Geneva I had discussed the matter with the Sudanese minister of education and the permanent representative to the United Nations in Geneva, a prominent figure in the National Islamic Front. Both men had said the international community needed to develop mechanisms to protect the internally displaced that would be comparable to those developed for refugees after World War II. In my meetings with the various regional groups in Geneva, the Sudanese representative had voiced the same view, which had thereby become the official position of the Sudan. However, because I was aware of the mutability of diplomatic representation, I sought an affirmation of that policy to be reflected by government representatives to the pertinent forums of the UN system.

These objectives provided the visit with a framework for discussions with government officials, who pledged to support my mandate and facilitated my visits to the camps and Abyei. Although my plans also included seeing camps in Kadugli and Meirem in the western region of Kordofan, logistical and time constraints made that impossible. My visit was widely covered by the government-controlled media, which seemed to see it as an opportunity for improving the Sudan's international reputation on human rights, a move that aroused fears of opposition groups and others concerned with the performance of the government that the regime's human rights record was being whitewashed.

Although these political actions and reactions clouded the visit, the program and the discussions were a considerable success. I was enthusiastically welcomed by the displaced people in the camps, not only as a Sudanese national but as a symbol of the international concern for their plight. I was carried on shoulders by the crowd, as joyous chanting and singing filled the air. Sudanese officials who accompanied me, seeing a public relations coup in the demonstrations, proudly described the services provided for the displaced by the government and nongovernmental organizations, including Christian and Islamic relief agencies. The aid covered maternity care, early child care, immunization, meals programs for small children, general medical care, education, and food distribution. Considering that the Sudan is a poor country in which such services are not easily available to many communities under normal conditions, what was being done seemed impressive, and I said so. The dwellings, which were built by the displaced themselves from local materials, did not differ from those often found in the shantytowns in which they had lived around Khartoum, although they were spread out more. The officials defended the resettlement policy by pointing to the contrast between how the displaced now lived and what they described as the dehumanizing conditions in the squalid areas of the industrial periphery of Khartoum-North.

People at the camps, however, far away from home and evicted from the city, revealed an unmistakable resentment at the inherently degrading conditions of their displacement. Behind the superficially happy faces was a sense of rejection, uprootedness, alienation, and anxiety, a suspension between despair and hope, all of which they communicated by various means, mostly in Dinka. One person spoke as the crowd watched approvingly: "We will not tell you anything; you watch with your own eyes, then go and think for yourself."

I was made to doubt whether all that officials described as being done was in fact being done. In one of the camps, after receiving an elaborate explanation of the health services being delivered, I asked the staff if they had any problems. The answer, which clearly embarrassed the officials with me, was, "We have no medicines." Referring to the health services, one Dinka said, "Do not believe what you hear; our babies are all finished with death." A third man, who would not stop complaining, much to the annoyance of a relative who accompanied me, said, "I am speaking my mind because someone must; I know that I will not remain free after you go." I wondered later whether I would protect or expose him if I raised his concern with the authorities. I chose silence. And indeed, my annoyed relative meant to protect him when he said impatiently, "Do you have to keep repeating yourself, when you have already been heard?"

People in the camps and others I encountered in the city remarked in almost coded language, "We should cut it," meaning that the South and the North should be separated. People stuffed written complaints into my pockets without even drawing my attention. And a pile of papers and messages, which I could not find time to read, accumulated in my hotel room, to be at last sorted out with the help of trusted people the night of my departure. For these among other reasons, the visits to the camps left me with mixed feelings, despite my overall view that the experience generated a constructive dialogue with the authorities.

The officials had earlier shown me the results of surveys they had conducted at the camps to make the point that although most of the displaced had initially wanted to return to the South, the overwhelming majority now favored remaining in the camps, an attitude the authorities welcomed as auguring well for national integration. My field impressions demonstrated the barriers that separated the rulers from the people, as I observed a clear tension, bordering on animosity, among most people at the camp and southern sympathizers in the city, some of whom were afraid, perhaps misguided by what they saw or heard through the media, that I was missing the authentic southern point of view. Ironically, some of the southerners most critical of the regime's policies were well placed within the system, clearly reflecting divided loyalties between the government they served and the rebel movement that they also saw as fighting for their cause.

In Abyei, on the North-South border, where the people were either indigenous or were close to their original homes further south, conditions contrasted sharply with those in the camps around Khartoum. (Because I come from the Dinka of Abyei, I had felt the same trepidations about visiting the area that I had felt about including the Sudan on my international mission. But I had chosen to visit for the same reasons I had chosen to visit the Sudan and with the same awareness of the risks involved to the integrity of my mission and my responsibility for even-handedness toward all concerned.) Although relief supplies had not arrived because Abyei is isolated from the rest of the country during the rainy season, the local population had managed to survive by cultivating land (within the territorial restrictions imposed by their security concerns) or by gathering seeds from the roots of the water lilies and other wild food. They were unequivocal in their welcome, in expressing their appreciation to the secretary-general for the concern demonstrated by the international community, and in their reaction to the government for facilitating my visit. Their public display of happiness was unprecedented in my memory of the area. This did not mean that they were happier but only that the occasion gave them hope.

The contrast with the camps was not so much that the people in Abyei were better provided for but that in comparison they enjoyed at least some security, dignity, and autonomy, although many wondered how long these would last in view of the war dangers looming nearby. Abyei has indeed had a long history of being a link between the North and South—often a bridge for peaceful interaction, sometimes a point of confrontation. The area had been among those hardest hit by Arab tribal militias and the mass starvation of the late 1980s. Relations had, however, improved significantly, as the Arab tribes, from which militias had been recruited by the government of the parliamentary democracy, considered themselves more on an equal footing with the Dinka under the military rule and also feared reprisals by the SPLA. Furthermore, the military regime adopted policies that were restoring confidence in traditional leaders who were assuming a greater role in preserving security. Under their respective traditional leaderships, the Dinka and the Arabs of southern Kordofan once again saw mutual advantage in resorting to their tribal diplomacy and the long-tested principles of good neighborliness.

Several conclusions emerged from the contrast between the camps and Abyei, which I presented to the government for policy considerations and which were, on the whole, well received. First, whatever services were being rendered, the location of the displaced just outside Khartoum, where they were neither part of the urban community nor in their own natural setting, was inherently degrading, especially since it was popularly believed that they had been removed to cleanse the city of undesirable non-Muslim elements. Second, the fact that their shanty dwellings in the camps were not better than those they lived in before, except for a more open barren space, did not adequately compensate for their removal from the city.

I recommended that as much as possible people be given the choice and assisted to go back to their areas of origin or to settlements close to them. They should also be accorded the protection and assistance necessary to resume normal, self-sustaining rural life. Those who choose not to go back should be assisted to move freely anywhere in the country, including urban centers, and given the necessary assistance to become ordinary integrated citizens. Those who choose to remain in the camps should not only be given the services of the kind described to me but should be assisted with materials to build more comfortable and healthier accommodations to help compensate for their isolation. Organizations that rendered services to the displaced had erected for themselves facilities that were attractive, even though they were inexpensively built from local materials. Extending such expertise to the displaced and helping them help themselves would seem a feasible and inexpensive way to achieve a humanitarian objective.

Several improvements were suggested concerning the delivery of needed relief supplies to Abyei. A number of the governmental and nongovernmental agencies that accompanied me on the visit to Abyei later met and pledged to deliver more agricultural equipment, medical supplies, and food. The Foundation for Peace and Development, a government institution, requested international cooperation in constructing an all-weather road to link Abyei with Muglad to the north to break the isolation of the area during the rainy season and maintain a steady flow of supplies. The foundation also appealed for international support to implement various projects for the displaced, in particular to provide housing. Subject to further consultations, a preliminary understanding was reached with the foundation that an international conference on the displaced in the Sudan be organized in cooperation with the United Nations and other international agencies.

I later shared these ideas with representatives of the international donor community in Khartoum, who, while expressing skepticism based on past experience, welcomed the dialogue with the government. They also expressed their desire to support some of the measures, such as the willing or free return of the displaced to their areas of origin and the organization of an international conference on the internally displaced, subject, of course, to the reaction of their capitals and the availability of resources.

I also held a meeting with nongovernmental organizations and, at its request, separately with the Sudan Council of Churches to discuss the problems of the internally displaced and the services extended to them. The Sudan Council of Churches, which had been involved in earlier projects for returnees, was expected to be among the nongovernmental organizations that might apply for support to assist those wishing to return to their homes.

My meeting with the minister of justice revealed important problems the internally displaced confront in the justice system that urgently need remedial measures. The minister informed me that he and the chief justice, on a visit to one of the central prisons in the capital, had come across a large number of southerners who had been kept in custody for long periods without trial or even charges. They immediately ordered them to be released without worrying about the legal basis for their order. I recalled to the minister reports I had received when I was in government from public figures who, while in detention, had found southerners under the same conditions. I urged the minister to do more than empty only one prison of southern victims of miscarriages of justice. If he were to make that a national campaign, he would make a major contribution to the administration of justice in the Sudan. The minister clearly appreciated the point and agreed in principle to do something. At least, as he put it, he could initiate a review of conditions in prisons to determine how widespread the problem was.

Although the steps that were agreed on with the government authorities were small in relation to the needs of internally displaced persons, the understandings emphasized the potential of a functional mandate that would encourage further dialogue. Both the under secretary-general for humanitarian affairs, who had also visited the Sudan, and his deputy in Geneva, who was about to visit, were briefed and undertook follow-up measures, which further emphasizes this potential. Of course, the secretary-general was also fully briefed on the visit. It is hoped that the government authorities will carry out measures to improve the situation of the displaced persons in accordance with the intentions stated during our discussions and that the measures will have value beyond a symbolic gesture and improved public relations.

An overarching reality of the situation in the Sudan, however, is that the matters discussed cover only minor aspects of a much larger crisis of displacement affecting millions of people in the war-ravaged zones, especially in the South. The quest for peace was nearly always spotlighted as the core issue. One of the school children's songs at Dar-es-Salaam camp included the words "Give us peace." With an exaggeration of what people expected my mission to accomplish, one elder at the Jebel Awlia camp said, "The best relief assistance you can give us is peace."

The options available to the parties appear to have crystallized, which may make it easier to negotiate a settlement. To achieve this, the Sudan will need a third party to facilitate a compromise. At present, the government appears to be torn between wanting a solution by the Sudanese themselves and needing third parties to break the impasse. The government also appears poised between a genuine yearning for peace and an unwavering commitment to Sharia. All the factions of the SPLM-SPLA seem equally committed to their objectives, especially to a secular state. This combination makes compromise difficult. But the clarity of vision on both sides also makes the issues obvious. How these positions can be reconciled is the challenge confronting the Sudan and all men and women of good will.

At the moment, each side tries to divide and weaken the other, both politically and militarily. The government seeks to drive wedges between the factions of the SPLM-SPLA, and the movement seeks to ally with opposition groups in the North. As I pointed out to government officials and to the leadership of the SPLM-SPLA, these divisive maneuvers may be beneficial for the short-term tactical purposes, but they cannot move the nation toward peace and unity. Internal unity within both the North and the South should be a first step toward unity of the North and the South and is therefore a prerequisite for peace. What the Sudan needs is a statesmanlike vision with which all Sudanese could identify as a framework for just and equitable participation in public life.

Despite the recent victories of the government forces in battle, it is widely recognized, even by the government itself, that the issues involved cannot ultimately be resolved by war. Indeed, although the recent disunity in the SPLM-SPLA may weaken the movement, the cause of the South is too deeply rooted to be eradicated by force. The real danger now looming in the societies of the southern Sudan, which like Somali society are based on a segmentary lineage system with the potential for divisiveness, is that fragmentation will increase so much it could prove very difficult and costly to manage. Unless the Sudan can bring a speedy end to the conflict and reconstruct the country through an all-inclusive peace and respect for all racial, ethnic, cultural, linguistic, and religious groups, the problem of the internally displaced and of human rights violations in general may prove daunting for the country and the international community.

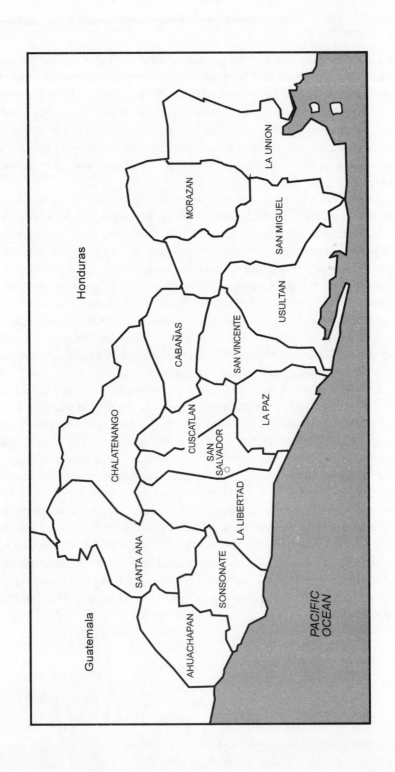

5

El Salvador:
Peace in the Balance

El Salvador was different from the other countries I visited because for the most part it has been a model of close cooperation between a troubled country and the international community, not only to achieve internal peace but to consolidate that peace by establishing a self-sustaining democracy. The peace agreement of January 16, 1992, that ended twelve years of civil war was negotiated under the auspices of the United Nations. It laid out reforms aimed at permitting the opposition Farabundo Marti Liberation Front (FMLN) to participate in the political life of the country, a participation that has transformed the institutions responsible for major violations of human rights and achieved greater justice in the social and economic life of the country.

By the time the 1992 peace accords were signed, the civil war in El Salvador had cost $6 billion, displaced one-quarter of the population, and killed 75,000 citizens.[1] Consequently, if successfully implemented, the accords promise not only a higher standard of respect for human rights and a major step in rebuilding El Salvador but could present a pattern for conflict resolution in the post–cold war era, a pattern in which strategic concerns can be separated from local political consequences. Significantly, any success toward this ambitious end will be predicated on addressing two crucial legacies of El Salvador's past: badly skewed land distribution and tenure (and resultant socioeconomic issues) and the absence of a representative and legitimate civilian police force.

---

1. Terry Lynn Karl, "El Salvador's Negotiated Revolution," *Foreign Affairs*, vol. 71 (Spring 1992), p. 164.

Background

The arrival and settlement of Spanish conquistadors in the middle of the sixteenth century disrupted indigenous social and political systems throughout Central and South America in a way that was to have far-reaching consequences. In what eventually became El Salvador the colonists confronted a native society characterized by hierarchical tribal structures organized around the communal ownership of land.[2] During the next century the colonists transformed the society and economy of the region into a semifeudal system of relatively self-sufficient haciendas (plantations) that controlled large tracts of land used for cattle breeding and cultivating some cash crops. In the process they created a Spanish-speaking, mixed-race (mestizo) peasantry that by the middle of the twentieth century would comprise more than 90 percent of the total population. The creation of this overwhelming majority helped mitigate the ethnic and racial hostilities that European hegemony often inflamed in other colonial territories.

But as the ethnic composition of the population became more uniform, land ownership was becoming increasingly concentrated. By the time independence was declared in 1821, one-third of the total land area was controlled by 400 large haciendas. Burgeoning wealth brought class distinctions, social control, and eventually political power. By the late nineteenth century the "Fourteen Families" had effectively seized control of the state: most presidents were major coffee growers and high-ranking military officers (these same families continued to control El Salvador's economy until the 1980s).[3] Meanwhile, the conditions of the average Salvadoran deteriorated. A century after independence, one commentator angrily criticized the social cleavages of the system in terms often echoed by Salvadorans today: "The conquest of territory by the coffee industry is alarming. It is extended like the conquistador, spreading hunger and misery, reducing the former proprietors to the worst conditions. . . . What good does it do to make money from the sale of coffee when it leaves so many people in misery?"[4]

2. Tommie Sue Montgomery, *Revolution in El Salvador: Origins and Evolution* (Boulder, Colo.: Westview Press, 1982), p. 33.

3. Montgomery, *Revolution in El Salvador*, p. 42.

4. "La Crisis del Maiz," *Patria*, January 18, 1929, quoted in Montgomery, *Revolution in El Salvador*, pp. 46–47.

Despite the development of strong, Marxist-oriented labor unions and intermittent and often violent peasant revolts, the elite were unwilling to share power. A turning point in the country's history came on December 2, 1931, when a military coup ousted freely elected President Arturo Araujo. Although himself a wealthy landowner and member of the country's social oligarchy, Araujo had come to power with the support of popular organizations and seemed inclined to implement some economic and political reforms. His overthrow by powerful military generals not only anticipated the nature of the conflict to come, but crystallized the issues of inadequate democratic participation, violations of human rights, and unfair land distribution that eventually determined its resolution. Of the event's significance in terms of the detachment of civil society from the state, one historian said that before December 2 the "forces of the oligarchy were thrown into the struggle for power, organizing more or less successful parties and electoral movements, exciting the masses; afterwards the entire oligarchy withdrew from the political game in order to leave it to military tyranny. . . . [The military] was transformed, in practice, into the great elector and into a type of political party permanently in arms."[5]

The most deadly phase of the El Salvadoran conflict originated in a similar dynamic as rightist military officers attempted to block land and other reforms by taking control of a progressive military coup in October 1979. This time, however, as the state once again used its security forces to consolidate power and exclude popular movements on the left from political participation, it was confronted with ferocious and increasingly organized resistance. In October 1980 a coalition of five armed communist revolutionary groups formed the FMLN; by 1983, in alliance with local communities, it had gained the military advantage. As the fabric of Salvadoran society unraveled, the Reagan administration, apprehensive over the alliance between the FMLN and the leftist Nicaraguan Sandinistas, intervened. The United States poured $1.8 million into El Salvador's 1984 presidential elections to guarantee the victory of Christian Democrat José Napoleon Duarte, then supplied his regime up to $1.2 million a day to continue the anticommunist war against the FMLN.[6]

5. Montgomery, *Revolution in El Salvador*, p. 53.
6. Karl, "El Salvador's Negotiated Revolution," p. 150.

Throughout the 1980s, human rights abuses, activated by historical class enmities and aggravated by cold war politics, escalated. Summary executions, extrajudicial detentions, torture, and wholesale massacres were perpetrated by both government death squads and guerilla forces.[7] And as in civil wars elsewhere, civilian populations thought to be sympathetic to the enemy were particular targets of killings and torture in a policy of "draining the sea to leave the fish."[8] By the mid-1980s the Salvadoran armed forces, reportedly with U.S. encouragement, discontinued major search-and-destroy military missions, adopting instead a low-intensity strategy in which they increasingly used the disruption or destruction of food supplies as a weapon, obstructed relief supplies to beleaguered communities, and denied hundreds of thousands of people freedom of movement and residence. The policy had two objectives: "to prevent independent organizations from promoting the wholesale repopulation of areas that were depopulated for military reasons, and . . . to prevent the consolidation of existing repopulated communities in order to make them dependent for survival on military benevolence."[9]

By the end of the decade, after more than 20 percent of Salvadorans had been forced to flee to neighboring Honduras and Nicaragua, the antagonists found themselves at a political as well as a military stalemate. The government insisted on the immediate disarming of the FMLN and on unconditional acceptance of the 1983 constitution, which the rebels considered inadequate, particularly on the issue of land reform in the rebel-held areas.[10] In return the FMLN demanded the abolition of the constitution, wholesale reorganization of the military establishment, and reiterated its long-standing call for new power-sharing arrangements to be determined by a provisional government charged with overseeing the transition to multiparty elections.

The electoral defeat of the Sandinistas in Nicaragua on February 25, 1990, and the more pragmatic orientation of a Bush administration

7. Americas Watch, *Nightmare Revisited: 1987–88* (Washington: Human Rights Watch, September 1988). For a full account of El Salvador's human rights record in the 1980s see Americas Watch, *El Salvador's Decade of Terror: Human Rights since the Assassination of Archbishop Romero* (Yale University Press, 1991).
8. Peter Sollis, "Displaced Persons and Human Rights: the Crisis in El Salvador," *Bulletin of Latin American Research*, vol. 11 (January 1992), p. 49.
9. Sollis, "Displaced Persons," p. 3.
10. For more on the land reform debate see Robert S. Leiken and Barry Rubin, eds., *The Central American Crisis Reader* (Summit Books, 1987), pp. 342–47.

unburdened by fading cold war concerns combined to assist in breaking the political impasse. In October 1990 the U.S. Congress, appalled by the human rights abuses in the country and especially the murder of six Jesuit priests by U.S.-trained army officers, slashed military aid to the government by 50 percent.[11] This tilted the balance in favor of peace.

With domestic and international opinion strongly supporting negotiations, FMLN leaders distanced themselves from the rhetoric of socialism and radical economic reform in favor of the principles of democratic pluralism. President Alfredo Cristiani of the ruling Nationalist Republican Alliance (ANERA) and a number of the more powerful business and military leaders expressed their support for a negotiated settlement and a modicum of political and economic reform. A genuine compromise seemed possible, if not imminent, as both sides met in Geneva under the guidance of the United Nations in April 1990. Two years later, after a number of setbacks, a comprehensive peace settlement was signed. Among other reforms it provided for demobilizing both the army and the guerrillas, dismantling the dreaded security forces, establishing a neutral judicial system, and altering electoral laws so as to allow all Salvadorans to participate in the political process. Nevertheless, as one scholar has noted, a "decade of conflict has altered civil society and irreversibly mobilized many groups previously marginalized from politics."[12] Consequently, if the peace accord does not adequately address the underlying political and economic causes of the conflict, these new social forces could undermine all efforts aimed at rebuilding the state.[13]

Observations

As guarantor of general security, the United Nations has so far played a crucial role in confidence building among Salvadoran parties and, in the words of one expert, has demonstrated that "support for multilateral negotiations can be more effective and less costly than the unilateral use

11. Karl, "El Salvador's Negotiated Revolution," p. 156.
12. Forrest D. Colburn, "The Fading of the Revolutionary Era in Central America," *Current History* (February 1992), p. 71.
13. Reporting on the fragility of the cease-fire agreement, Douglas Farah reiterated that the issues demanding the most concessions from both sides are disarmament of the FMLN (which so far has demobilized only 40 percent of its forces), restructuring of the army, and electoral and legal reforms. See "Crisis Grips Salvadoran Peace Process," *Washington Post*, October 25, 1992, p. A29.

of force."[14] The factors influencing the government to favor peace included the stalemate in the war, the weariness of the U.S. Congress at pouring money into the country, international concern about human rights abuses, and the reduction of U.S. military aid. On the part of the FMLN, the loss of the pressure against El Salvador from Nicaragua and of support from Cuba were said to be pivotal. U.S. support for the UN-sponsored talks and the inclusion of other countries from the region greatly facilitated ending the war. Yet although some important strides were made in peace negotiations, particularly on electoral reform and purging the security forces, unless agrarian reform and socioeconomic inequities among El Salvador's displaced and refugee populations are adequately addressed, there can be little hope for lasting peace.

Displacement, the direct consequence of insurgency and counterinsurgency, meant that the social fabric was torn, family bonds broken, economic structures destroyed, and peasants uprooted from their way of life. It had changed people's self-perceptions, introduced new values, and sharpened poverty. Civil society had collapsed. By 1984 some 70 percent of the population in the war zone had fled to the slums around urban centers or across the borders into neighboring countries. With the war continuing and the hardships of displacement intensifying, those who had left began to return and repopulate the rural areas, and brought with them more tragedy.

Because displacement had largely been the result of the conflict and the warring parties' brutality toward the civilian population, the peace accords have considerably improved the observance of human rights. In meetings I held with intergovernmental organizations, nongovernmental organizations in San Salvador, and rural populations in Usulutan and Cuscatian (which were among the most affected by the war), all expressed deep appreciation for the protection of the UN observer mission (ONUSAL) and the presence of the High Commissioner for Refugees. They forcefully argued that the UN presence was crucial to the cause of peace and the observation of human rights, that international access to the vulnerable population was vital to their protection and self-reliance, and that, although the invitation or at least the consent of host countries was a necessary condition, the international community should not be passive about its protective role. The government also accepted the

14. Karl, "El Salvador's Negotiated Revolution," p. 164.

presence of the United Nations through its agencies as necessary for development.

The president of the community at Usulutan, a middle-aged man who said he did not know why he had been elected since he could not write or read, explained that the military authorities had treated people in rural areas as subversives and that the Catholic church had also been implicated. Educated people in particular, some of whom had studied in Mexico, were kidnapped and killed. As the conflict intensified, many went underground, and the community felt obligated to protect them. In reaction, the authorities embarked on a policy of indiscriminate brutality against the community. The result was that "no one spoke the truth" because "it was a crime to speak the truth." Explaining the hardships the peasants endured during the war, he said, "our crime was that we are poor." Yet another crime, he argued, was to have remained in the area. Massive troop deployments attempted to sweep the insurgency away. Food had to be buried or the army would destroy it. Sometimes people hid underground for weeks with children crying. People were captured at random, taken away, and killed. "It was a bad treatment," he said quietly.

He saw little improvement in his people's sense of dignity in refugee camps, where they were fed but could not produce anything. This was what made them eventually return to their villages despite the dangers. Confronted by the army on their return, they were detained and the foreigners accompanying them were physically abused. Lack of documentation made it difficult for the peasants to assert their rights of citizenship. As though to reassure himself that his own moral code had not been destroyed, the president went on to say, "I believe in God and in humanity. I do not hate anyone, whether he is a guerilla or a government soldier. What I hate are bad actions, whoever they come from."

Among the specific problems leading to the conflict, he highlighted the lack of land: "People do not have even a piece of land on which to grow the corn they need for their own food." He prayed for a new El Salvador and for development programs that would benefit all people. In that respect, "everything goes back to the inequities of ownership and use of the land." The causes of the war were deeply rooted in economic disparities. The peasants had no education, health services, or development programs, and they suffered from violations of human rights.

The president of the community welcomed the peace accords and the prospects they offered to the rural people. They needed education, health services, and help in developing a community that was economically, socially, and culturally self-reliant. The principles of the Universal Declaration of Human Rights, he said, seemed too removed from conditions in El Salvador, where poverty prevented people from understanding their rights under the national constitution, much less under international agreements. The nongovernmental organizations and the international community as a whole were not only needed helpers but also protectors. He pleaded for a permanent UN representative to monitor human rights violations and fill the vacuum of protection that he feared would be created by the withdrawal of the UN observer mission.

Another spokesman pointed to the unequal distribution of power, the neglect of rural people, and discrimination in education, health services, and housing as major causes of the conflict. The credit system was in the hands of big business, he said, and was always promoting the goals of big business, which were focused abroad. Traditional political parties always tried to get things for the people they represented who could vote them in and out of power. Because rural and urban poor people lacked political power and had no appeal for politicians, they were ignored. Those who sought to get some power "for the dispossessed" were opposed by the military and the security forces.

The peace accords were the most promising development in the country, he said. The terms of the accords confirmed that the discrimination they complained about indeed existed. However, he expressed concern about implementation. The authorities were procrastinating in implementing reform of the agricultural credit system, redeployment of the armed forces, establishment of a civilian police force, and redistribution of land.

Perhaps the subject that preoccupied rural people the most was the prospect that the international community might abandon them. Rumors that UNHCR and even ONUSAL would soon withdraw from El Salvador triggered fears that hostilities could resume and the brutalities would return. Pleas for the continued presence of the United Nations and international nongovernmental organizations were blazoned on banners, prepared by spokespersons, and presented in statements submitted to me. The sentiments had much in common with those I had heard before, especially about conditions in the southern Sudan.

More often than anywhere else, however, the needy people of rural El Salvador saw the causes of the conflict and their plight as poverty. And indeed, conditions in the areas I visited were dismally poor by any standards. Development experts explained that 70 percent to 80 percent of the people in Central America were on the verge of poverty, that the governments were generally right wing, and that their economic programs did not much benefit the poor. Costa Rica was cited as the only exception. The most urgent matter of concern for the rural poor was the sensitive issue of land reform. Second was the lack of documentation resulting from the disappearance of birth certificates, identity cards, tax cards, and electoral cards. Many rural people had been uprooted by the war, fled to neighboring countries, and later returned to their villages, losing or being deprived of identification along the way. Without identity cards, it was legally impossible for them to exercise the political and economic rights of citizenship.

Discussions with the minister of foreign affairs, the deputy minister, and other government officials were cordial and candid. While confirming that El Salvador was a model of international cooperation on a domestic problem, they considered the presence of ONUSAL, desirable and welcome as it was, temporary and thought it should end as soon as circumstances permitted.

They viewed internal displacement as a passing problem that was already being resolved. While it persisted, they questioned the disproportionate distribution of assistance—some areas received massive aid and others were totally neglected. They said the objective should be to provide uniform assistance to all the needy. To do that systematically, they believed it was more constructive to use government institutions instead of parallel nongovernmental entities to distribute services. I tried to explain that NGO activities were intended to complement government efforts, especially where parts of the population were neglected either willfully or because of lack of government resources. And these organizations provided practical means of reaching the rural masses who sometimes fell outside a government's reach. In that sense, they offered a channel for a more equitable distribution of aid. And in fact, discussions with nongovernmental organizations in San Salvador, some of whose representatives accompanied me to the field, and with the peasants showed considerable mutual trust. The NGOs appeared to represent the interests of the rural poor.

In light of the country's history, it seemed appropriate that government officials chose to address internal problems as a consequence of poverty. They attributed the country's absence of ethnic animosities to historical racial and ethnic melding. Their emphasis on the implicit class conflict in El Salvador offers a useful contrast to the emphasis on ethnicity as the principal factor in internal conflicts elsewhere. Whether or not ethnicity is a factor, the Marxist insistence on class conflict as a cause of civil strife suggests that the root of internal conflict may not be diversity as such but rather the implications of diversity for general participation in political decisions and equitable distribution of resources.

Salvadoran authorities, representatives of UN bodies, and NGOs all pointed to the International Conference on Refugees in Central America (CIREFCA) as a comprehensive plan for treating the problems of refugees and displaced persons on the basis of need. Assistance and protection do not depend on whether the people are refugees or internally displaced persons. CIREFCA was conceived as a program for assisting refugees, but separating aid for refugees from aid for those who were in need but could not qualify as refugees proved exceedingly difficult. The concept of the CIREFCA population, which did not discriminate, was thus a way to provide assistance to all needy people. Indeed, the CIREFCA process of identification and assistance was often cited in other discussions in El Salvador as a model of effective regional cooperation on the problems of displacement.

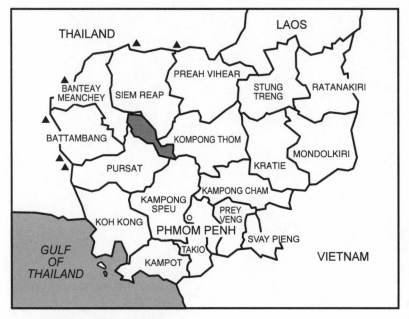

▲ THAI BORDER CAMPS

6

Cambodia:
Rebuilding a Nation

A long with Somalia, Cambodia has been labeled a failed state: despite freedom from colonial rule, it can be considered self-governing only in a technical sense.[1] Twenty years of civil war, invasions, destruction of infrastructure, gross violations of human rights, and massive dislocations among its people have rendered the country ungovernable. Cambodia's suffering began in 1970, when it was embroiled in the devastation of the Vietnam War and ravaged by U.S. bombing. The devastation continued through years of civil war wrought by the communist Khmer Rouge (1975–78), the invasion and occupation by Vietnam (1978–89), and the war of resistance against the Vietnamese occupiers and the government they installed (1979–93). The result has been the deaths of 2 million to 3 million Cambodians and the displacement of hundreds of thousands.

The Khmer Rouge regime was particularly harsh. Inspired by an extreme version of the agrarian communism of Mao Zedong, the regime violently suppressed all forms of dissent and expression, depopulated entire cities, and conducted mass executions in attempts to control all aspects of social life. Vietnam's invasion of Cambodia in December 1978 and its installation of a satellite regime in Phnom Penh brought some relief. It ended Khmer Rouge rule and introduced conciliatory policies, including the dissolution of large labor camps, reunion of divided families, and restoration of basic services such as education and health care. But in pursuing the retreating Khmer Rouge forces in 1979, the Vietnam-

1. Gerald B. Helman and Steven R. Ratner, "Saving Failed States," *Foreign Policy*, no. 89 (Winter 1992-93), p. 17.

ese army adopted a scorched earth policy, creating famine that killed tens of thousands and forced 360,000 Cambodian refugees to settle along the border with Thailand.[2]

As refugees filled border camps, the various anti-Vietnam factions (in addition to the Khmer Rouge) set up bases in those camps.[3] These factions systematically violated the human rights of civilians in attempts to establish a presence in Cambodia and bolster their political legitimacy. They also impeded the efforts of the United Nations and other international aid agencies to deliver relief supplies and repatriate hundreds of thousands of refugees. The most serious human rights violations occurred in areas controlled by the Khmer Rouge, who denied refugees food and medical care and forcibly conscripted children into their ranks.[4] Continued military conflict has led to the internal displacement of 180,000 Cambodians. An estimated 200,000 soldiers scheduled for demobilization brings the total to more than 700,000 that must be resettled. This represents one of the largest mass movements of people in recent history.

Many factors have contributed to the breakdown of Cambodia's social order. The country's history has been characterized by shifting external rivalries and domestic conflict. These have made it very difficult for contending Cambodian parties to conceive of their survival within the context of genuine power sharing. Long before the international conference on Cambodia convened in Paris on July 30, 1991, it was clear that the magnitude of the country's problems would require any durable peace to encompass not only a cessation of hostilities but a comprehensive plan of social and economic reconstruction.

2. Stephen J. Morris, "Vietnam's Vietnam," *Atlantic Monthly*, January 1985, p. 1; and Frank Frost, "The Cambodian Conflict: The Path Towards Peace," *Contemporary Southeast Asia*, vol. 13 (September 1991), p. 21.

3. In addition to the Khmer Rouge, which survived the expulsion from Cambodia in part because of China's assistance, two other anticommunist factions emerged in opposition to the Vietnamese-installed regime of Hun Sen. In 1979 the Khmer People's National Liberation Front was established under the leadership of former Prime Minister Son Sann, and in 1981 Prince Norodom Sihanouk formed the United Front for an Independent, Neutral, Peaceful and Cooperative Cambodia.

4. Asia Watch, *Khmer Rouge Abuses along the Thai-Cambodian Border: An Asia Watch Report* (Washington: Human Rights Watch, February 1989).

Background

When the French colonized Cambodia in the nineteenth century, they assumed control of state institutions left over from what had been the Angkor Empire. Lasting from the ninth to the fourteenth centuries, Angkor civilization, defined by its dominant ethnic group, the Khmer, had established a strong economic base with a sophisticated irrigation system. This facilitated the development and entrenchment of hierarchical tribal structures presided over by the absolute rule of the *deva-raj*, or god-king.[5] The increasing wealth of the kingdom was thus promoted by a highly centralized state system held together, in part, by Buddhism that filtered from India through neighboring Siam (Thailand).

At its peak the Angkor kingdom stretched east as far as China and encompassed all of Siam and the southern regions of Vietnam and Laos. But by the nineteenth century the cultural and territorial integrity of the Khmer people had been repeatedly violated as the emerging states of Siam and later Vietnam defeated their armies and annexed their lands, often with the collaboration of Khmer princes.[6] Such incursions, in combination with the disruptive effects of French colonial rule and, in the modern era, the cold war, were instrumental in creating the Khmer Rouge and bringing about a calamitous revolution.

The French colonial experiment in Cambodia and the way independence was finally negotiated set the stage for the civil conflict that erupted after the overthrow of the country's aristocratic oligarchy in 1970. Although Cambodian society remained stratified throughout the colonial period, it demonstrated a cohesiveness engendered by the French colonialists' indirect, albeit resolute, authority and a strong tradition of allegiance to the king that dated back to the Angkor era.[7] "Unlike

5. For an excellent account of Cambodian history see Elizabeth Becker, *When the War Was Over: The Voices of Cambodia's Revolution and Its People* (Simon and Schuster, 1986).

6. According to William Shawcross, there was a vital difference in the Khmer people's relations with Thailand and Vietnam. The Khmers and Thais shared similar religious and cultural patterns that mitigated the effects of Thai occupation, but Vietnam's mixture of Indian-influenced and Chinese world views engendered much bitterness. See *Sideshow: Kissinger, Nixon and the Destruction of Cambodia* (Simon and Schuster, 1979), p. 41.

7. Cambodia was ruled as a French protectorate within the Union Indochinoise along with the territories of central and northern Vietnam. Southern Vietnam, however, was ruled directly as a French colony.

Vietnam and other countries of the Chinese tradition," one scholar has commented, "Cambodia had no powerful mandarin class, only an aristocratic oligarchy whose fortunes were largely controlled by the king."[8] The king cooperated openly with the French, whom he believed protected his regime against domestic opposition and the persistent territorial claims of Siam and Vietnam. The French created a stability that enabled the Cambodians to improve their standards of education and living, but ironically this advance led to the cultural revivalist movement and the ideological drive for an independent modern Khmer nation.[9]

Two other developments contributed to this nationalist drive: the Japanese occupation of Cambodia during World War II and the support of Vietnamese communists for the emerging Cambodian communist movement. The Japanese invasion in 1941 left Prince Norodom Sihanouk on the throne and the French in nominal control, but both the aristocratic oligarchy and the French "protectors" were discredited in the eyes of the Cambodian nationalists. By the end of 1944 the Japanese became increasingly concerned over the French administration's covert allegiance to the allies and decided to displace it. In March 1945 they persuaded Prince Sihanouk to proclaim his country's independence. They also allowed Thailand to annex a third of Cambodia's territory in return for its renunciation of sovereignty over Cambodia as a whole.[10] Meanwhile, deep inequities within society had given birth to the Khmer Rouge, who allied themselves with Ho Chi Minh and the founders of the Communist party in Vietnam.

After World War II, Cambodia once again became an associated state in the French Union of Indochina and was increasingly considered a bulwark against Hanoi and the spread of communist influence in southeast Asia. Determined to prevent the establishment of another radical regime in the region, the French secured Prince Sihanouk's position on the throne by establishing a constitutional monarchy and permitting some popular political activity. This led to tensions between the monarchy and the radical segments of society, who saw it as one more affront

8. Shawcross, *Sideshow*, p. 57.
9. Becker, *When the War Was Over*, pp. 53-58.
10. In 1867 the French ceded to Siam the provinces of Battambang and Angkor in return for Siamese renunciation of sovereignty over the rest of Cambodia. It was these same provinces, which the Cambodians had regained in 1907, that the Japanese insisted must revert once more to Thailand. When the French secured their return in 1946, Cambodia's prewar borders were restored, but neither Vietnam nor Thailand have ever respected them.

to the nationalist cause. In 1953, weary from a debilitating war in Vietnam and only marginally interested in Cambodia, the French negotiated the country's independence with Sihanouk, who subsequently declared himself the "father of independence." Two years later, in pursuit of greater legitimacy, he abdicated as hereditary monarch and became political leader of the newly formed People's Socialist Community party. In 1960 he was named head of state of the Republic of Cambodia and for almost a decade frustrated the aspirations of the communists by coopting many of their top leaders. Yet despite being widely accepted by the Cambodians as the father of the country, Sihanouk made little effort to unite the nation, which caused increased dissatisfaction. Cambodia "remained a feudal kingdom in which various barons, war lords, and landowners ruled in their own fiefdoms, paying him tributes and recognition. His political organization . . . was little more than a loose coalition of powerful families and cliques of different ideologies."[11] Nevertheless, Sihanouk, a savvy politician, continued to rule, in large part by following a policy of strict neutrality in foreign affairs, playing Vietnam and the United States (now increasingly involved in southeast Asia) against one another, and pursuing a carrot-and-stick policy toward the opposition at home.

If Sihanouk held Cambodia together, he also initiated its collapse. Between 1963 and 1970 his policy of state-sponsored terror involving widespread arrests and executions of suspected dissidents led hundreds of students and professionals to join the communist guerrillas in the jungle.[12] As the increasingly powerful Khmer Rouge, supported by Vietnam, took control of much of the countryside, Sihanouk began to accommodate Hanoi, alarming the rightist elements in his regime and in the American administration who were convinced that he was favoring Viet Minh forces by allowing them refuge in the country. In March 1970 the right-wing prime minister, General Lon Nol, in coalition with the officer corps and many urban elites, overthrew Sihanouk.[13] At China's behest the prince then formed an alliance with the Khmer Rouge to oppose the

11. Shawcross, *Sideshow*, p. 50.
12. Sidney Jones and Dinah Pokemper, "Human Rights in Cambodia: Past, Present, and Future," in Frederick Z. Brown, ed., *Rebuilding Cambodia: Human Resources, Human Rights, and Law* (Johns Hopkins University Press, 1993), pp. 44–45.
13. Allegations of American complicity in the coup have long persisted, but no firm evidence has been uncovered.

new regime. From 1970 to 1975 Lon Nol was steadily supported by the United States, which dropped hundreds of tons of bombs on territory held by the Khmer Rouge.[14] Attacks by the Khmer Rouge, most against civilian targets, were equally ferocious. In just one communist bombardment of Phnom Penh, for example, 10,000 homes were destroyed.[15]

The overthrow of the Lon Nol regime in 1975, within weeks after the American withdrawal from Vietnam, was followed by four years of Khmer Rouge rule under its founder Pol Pot. By some estimates this harsh rule led to the deaths of 1 million Cambodians and the disappearance of 20 percent of the population, including 500,000 ethnic Vietnamese, who had first settled during the French colonial period.[16] Intent upon nothing less than the reestablishment of a "pure" Khmer society, the Khmer Rouge evacuated the urban centers, dispersing the people to agricultural labor camps deep in the interior. Temples were demolished, Buddhist monks killed or banished, and family ties repressed and often severed in service to the regime. Under Khmer Rouge rule the country's economic infrastructure was dismantled and much of the urban-based population obliterated, including most educated people. The holocaust was so all-consuming that after four years fewer than 50 doctors and only 5,000 teachers survived. The Khmer Rouge also introduced unprecedented racial divisiveness: they proclaimed that Cambodia's non-Khmer ethnic minorities (Chinese, Thais, and others) threatened the Khmer purity of the nation, which led to wholesale massacres.[17]

In 1979, after repeated Cambodian military incursions into Vietnam, ostensibly to defeat disaffected former Khmer Rouge members, Soviet-backed Vietnamese forces overthrew the Pol Pot regime. The Vietnamese installed a communist government with Khmer Rouge defectors Hun Sen as premier of the People's Republic of Kampuchea (renamed the State of Cambodia in 1989) and Heng Samrin as president of the People's

14. By 1973 much of the American bombing ceased as the U.S. Congress challenged the legality of the raids because the United States was not in a state of war with Cambodia.

15. Shawcross, *Sideshow*, p. 224.

16. Chet Atkins, "Cambodia's 'Peace': Genocide, Justice and Silence," *Washington Post*, January 26, 1992, p. C4. It should be noted, however, that thousands of ethnic Vietnamese were massacred under the regime of Lon Nol, who believed them to be Viet Cong sympathizers. See Jones and Pokemper, "Human Rights in Cambodia," p. 45.

17. U.S. Committee for Refugees, *Cambodians in Thailand: People on the Edge* (Washington, December 1985), p. 4.

Revolutionary Council. Far from benign, the invasion caused the displacement of 1 million Cambodians and Vietnamese.[18]

The United States, China, and the Soviet Union continued to employ proxy armies in their struggle for influence in the country. In a bizarre alliance, China and the United States supported the ousted Khmer Rouge and two other guerilla armies. A more predictable coalition between Vietnam and the Soviet Union backed the regime in Phnom Penh.[19] But the external geopolitical dynamics driving the Cambodian conflict collapsed in 1989 when Vietnam withdrew and the European Eastern bloc dissolved. The reduction of tensions between the United States and the former Soviet Union and between the former Soviet Union and China has improved the climate for a settlement to the Cambodian conflict.

By 1991, deprived of external support, the Cambodian government and a coalition of insurgent groups were forced to accept a UN-brokered settlement involving a monitored cease-fire and the creation of a transitional administration preparatory to holding free elections. On June 10, 1993, following UN-supervised elections, the royalist opposition party, the United National Front for an Independent, Neutral, Peaceful and Cooperative Cambodia (FUNCINPEC), loyal to Prince Sihanouk and headed by his son Prince Norodom Rannaridh, received 45.5 percent of the vote. The governing Cambodian People's Party (CPP) received 38.2 percent and immediately brought charges of massive voting irregularities, causing some CPP partisans led by Prince Norodom Chakrapong, another son of Prince Sihanouk, to announce the secession of several eastern provinces. But progress toward national reconciliation resumed and the threat of renewed civil war subsided when the two major parties agreed to share power in an interim government, with Prince Sihanouk retaining his position as head of state until the popularly elected National Assembly drafts a constitution. Also encouraging was the announcement by the Khmer Rouge, who had stated they would boycott the elections and had dropped out of the UN-sponsored peace process in 1992, that

18. Refugee Policy Group, *Cambodia: A Time for Return, Reconciliation, and Reconstruction* (Washington, October 1991), p. 4.

19. China worried about Vietnam's hegemony in Indochina and, encouraged by the United States, gave the decimated Khmer Rouge forces a new lease on life. Also supporting the Khmer Rouge were the countries of the Association of Southeast Asian Nations (Thailand, Malaysia, Singapore, Indonesia, the Philippines, and Brunei).

they would accept the power-sharing agreement and an offer from Prince Sihanouk to have their members serve as advisors to the interim government.[20] However, whether the various parties will be able to cooperate in institutionalizing political power in a way that will secure a lasting peace remains to be seen.

Observations

On October 23, 1991, following four years of negotiations, diplomats from eighteen countries, including the five permanent member countries of the Security Council, met with representatives of Cambodia's four contending factions in Paris and adopted the Agreement on a Comprehensive Political Settlement of the Cambodia Conflict designed to bring about Cambodia's recovery after two decades of war and social disruption. The country's tragic history required, in the words of the agreement, "special measures to assure protection of human rights, and the non-return to the policies and practices of the past."[21] The agreement established a peacekeeping organization, the UN Transitional Authority in Cambodia (UNTAC), investing it with unparalleled powers over the government installed by Vietnam in 1979, its affiliated Cambodian People's Party, and the three other competing factions: the Khmer Rouge's Party of Democratic Kampuchea (PDK), FUNCINPEC formed by Prince Sihanouk and headed by Prince Norodom Rannaridh, and the Khmer People's National Liberation Front (KPNLF) led by former Prime Minister Son Sann. UNTAC's mandate (endorsed by the four factions) covered a wide spectrum of activities that unlike peacekeeping arrangements elsewhere authorized it to exercise considerable oversight of civil administration and military matters.

The Paris agreement stipulated that Cambodian sovereignty would rest in a Supreme National Council, composed of representatives of all the factions, under the chairmanship of Prince Sihanouk.[22] The SNC, in turn,

---

20. Philip Shenon, "A Role for the Khmer Rouge," *New York Times*, June 26, 1992, p. A2.
21. Security Council, *The Situation in Cambodia*, A/46/61: S22059 (United Nations, January 1991), p. 4.
22. Formed in 1990, the SNC had six members from the government and two each from the three resistance factions.

delegated extensive powers to UNTAC, including lawmaking authority invested in a special representative of the secretary-general who would be responsible for determining matters of implementation whenever the council reached an impasse.[23]

In the first phase of the peace plan, UNTAC was authorized to supervise the cease-fire, verify the withdrawal of Vietnamese troops, disarm 70 percent of the warring parties' forces and place the rest in cantonments, and supervise the clearing of millions of land mines. The plan's broader goals—the achievement of a neutral political atmosphere conducive to the free and fair election of a constituent assembly, the drafting of a new constitution (after which the constituent assembly would be transformed into a legislative body), and the creation of a new Cambodian government—depended on the success of UNTAC's demobilization efforts and the cooperation of the various factions. To facilitate the impartiality of this process during the eighteen-month transition period, UNTAC was invited to place its own personnel in all of the key ministries, including defense, foreign affairs, finance, public security and information, and other government agencies relevant to the elections, the linchpin of the Paris agreement.[24]

The Paris agreement contained two further components related to human rights and the repatriation and resettlement of refugees and displaced persons. Article 14 makes UNTAC responsible during the transition period for "fostering an environment in which respect for human rights shall be ensured" in accordance with the rights and freedoms embodied in the Universal Declaration of Human Rights and other relevant international human rights instruments.[25] UNTAC was charged

23. The Paris agreement nominally preserved Cambodia's sovereignty during the transitional phase by stipulating that the United Nations must follow the instructions of the SNC when that body adopts positions unanimously or when it speaks in terms consistent, in the UN's opinion, with the agreements. Because it was unlikely that the warring factions would adopt unanimous positions on crucial matters, this meant that all authority was essentially given to the United Nations. In December 1991 Yasushi Akashi, a former Japanese diplomat, was appointed special representative of the secretary-general to direct the joint military-civilian UNTAC effort.

24. By September 1992 UNTAC had deployed 15,900 peacekeeping troops, 3,600 civilian police, and 3,000 civilian administrators and election officials. The operation cost an estimated $1.9 billion, not counting $600 million for the repatriation and resettlement by the UN High Commissioner for Refugees of 325,000 Cambodians living in camps in Thailand. See Frederick Z. Brown, "Cambodia in 1992: Peace at Peril," *Asian Survey*, vol. 33 (January 1993), pp. 84–85.

25. Security Council, *Situation in Cambodia*, part 3, article 15.

with developing and implementing a program of human rights education, investigating complaints, and taking corrective action when necessary. But no independent procedure for prosecution was established, nor were any other implementation mechanisms built into the agreement. This was partly because the military operation took increasing precedence and UNTAC's planners had not foreseen the important role the promotion of human rights would have, particularly with respect to creating a neutral political atmosphere before the elections and facilitating Cambodia's repatriation program.[26]

Under the Paris agreement, UNTAC was given responsibility for coordinating the repatriation and resettlement of refugees and displaced persons and affording them the "right to live in safety, security and dignity, free from intimidation or coercion of any kind."[27] This task, estimated to cost $600 million, was delegated to the UN High Commissioner for Refugees, which targeted two groups for assistance: the 360,000 Cambodian refugees living in camps along the Thai border and 180,000 displaced persons within Cambodia. By the end of 1992 more than half the people along the border had returned home. On March 30, 1993, one year after it began the repatriation program, the UNHCR closed its last Cambodian refugee camp in Thailand.

Refugees received travel assistance, some protection, and their choice of various kinds of resettlement aid. On the assumption that most of the people would return to their area of origin as farmers, the United Nations promised each person two hectares of land in addition to basic agricultural and household implements. However, because most returnees elected to settle in the fertile and densely populated Battambang province in the northwest rather than in their areas of origin, the UNHCR could not find sufficient mine-free arable land and had to reformulate its

26. Jarat Chopra, John Mackinlay, and Larry Minear, *Report on the Cambodian Peace Process*, no. 165 (Oslo: Norwegian Institute of International Affairs, February 1993), pp. 24–25. In a review of the UN operation, Human Rights Watch said that although UNTAC's presence in Cambodia has resulted in limited improvements, particularly in freedoms of association and speech, it has accorded a relatively low priority to human rights in the interest of keeping the peace process on track. In addition to citing the absence of qualified personnel and enforcement mechanisms to take corrective action once abuses have been investigated, Human Rights Watch also criticized the human rights component of the Paris accords for emphasizing human rights education over investigation and punishment. Human Rights Watch, *The Lost Agenda: Human Rights and UN Field Operations* (Washington, June 1993), pp. 37–74.
27. Security Council, *Situation in Cambodia*, part 5, article 20.

policy. It announced four options: two hectares of agricultural land, but not necessarily in the province of choice; a small plot of land and building materials to construct a home; a cash allowance of $50; or a technical assistance package to help start a small business. All the choices included a supply of food to last up to twelve months.[28] Despite these efforts to diversify the options, however, the slow pace of mine-clearing, disputes over land ownership, and the volume of returnees (30,000 a month) continue to make land scarce and have necessitated an intensified search for land in the center and east of the country.[29]

The internally displaced who are not returnees have not been the beneficiaries of any similarly focused international effort. Most fled their villages because of military conflict and live in camps. Others left out of fear of impending military attacks and live among relatives and friends. They took few personal possessions and, relative to the settled population, they have poorer shelter, more health problems, less education, and less revenue from agricultural production.[30] (To the extent that they may live in communities to which the refugees returned, they may share the benefits of improvements in water supplies, schools, and roads). But even though the cost of assisting the displaced population is small in comparison with the cost of assisting the refugees, funds have been slow in coming.[31]

Many Cambodians who had lived in the border camps and who had benefited from international aid programs for years returned to the same areas and to communities in which the internally displaced were located. Some refugees had received better health care and education than their new neighbors. UNTAC officials and associated nongovernmental organizations recognized the disparities and sought to plan communitywide activities to benefit both refugees and displaced persons. The distinctions, however, have proved difficult to erase. And there have been concerns that as the remainder of those abroad return, additional pressures on scarce land and social services may aggravate existing social

28. Asia Watch, *Political Control, Human Rights and the UN Mission in Cambodia* (Washington: Human Rights Watch, September 1992), p. 51.

29. Security Council, *Second Progress Report of the Secretary-General on the United Nations Transitional Authority in Cambodia*, S/24578 (September 1992), p. 11.

30. UN Transitional Authority in Cambodia (UNTAC), *The Secretary-General's Consolidated Appeal for Cambodia's Immediate Needs and National Rehabilitation* (May 1992), p. 13.

31. UNTAC, *Secretary-General's Consolidated Appeal*, p. 13.

tensions. These have already manifested themselves in increased anti-Vietnamese sentiment that the PDK (Khmer Rouge), seeking to present itself as the champion of Cambodian nationalism, has manipulated in its battle for control of the rural population. Premeditated massacres of ethnic Vietnamese have resulted, posing a grave threat to political reconciliation.[32]

Many observers, aid officials, and others have argued that if the international community had taken a more integrated institutional approach to meeting human needs and had not made invidious distinctions between internal and external displacement, social and economic reconstruction would be moving faster. The disparities between the international community's responses to refugees and internally displaced persons in similar circumstances and with similar needs is widely recognized as unfair. The Cambodian situation highlights the need for consistency in the design and implementation of humanitarian assistance and resettlement plans so as to reflect demonstrable needs rather than artificial geographic boundaries and labels.

---

32. Recently the Khmer Rouge exacerbated animosities by accusing the Vietnamese in Cambodia of seeking to colonize Khmer lands. "UN Says Khmer Rouge Killed 12 Ethnic Vietnamese," *New York Times*, December 30, 1992, p. A1.

Part II

Displacement in Global Perspective

7

The Challenge in the African Experience

More than 15 million of the 25 million displaced persons worldwide are from African countries with acute problems of nation building: crises of national identity and unity, ineffective government authority and control, limited capacity for economic productivity and resource distribution and, above all, tension between centralized political and economic forces and the demands of various constituencies for autonomy and equitable participation in political and economic life. Armed conflict among these constituencies has often erupted, and the resulting internally displaced exist in a vacuum of moral responsibility between contending forces, a vacuum for which the international community is called upon to compensate. To do this, of course, the community needs international legal standards and enforcement mechanisms, which are critically important to remedying the gross violations of human rights. But appreciating the underlying causes of the conflicts, addressing the problems at their domestic roots, and initiating ameliorative actions before problems reach the crisis level are crucial to achieving enduring solutions.

The Tension between Unity and Autonomy

When massive displacements occur, providing emergency relief becomes the immediate preoccupation. But in the longer term, relief must be combined with measures to protect human rights and strategies to address the underlying causes of displacement. Reconciling universal standards and internal dynamics calls for widening the global consensus supporting democratic ideals and respect for human dignity. Unless a government's perspective agrees with and reinforces universal standards, it cannot be sustainable in a world increasingly consciousness of human rights violations. This tension between local and global perspectives lies at the heart of the controversy on national sovereignty. As the Persian Gulf conflict, the wars in the former Yugoslavia, and the landing of U.S. troops in Somalia have shown, the right of sovereignty within national borders has become an ever more pressing issue.

The world seems to be of two minds simultaneously moving in opposite directions regarding the importance of national borders. On the one hand there are trends, such as in the European Community, toward overriding national borders to achieve a larger unity. On the other hand there are trends toward fragmentation, whereby new and sometimes deadly borders are erected within old states, as happened in the Soviet Union and Yugoslavia.

In *An Agenda for Peace*, UN Secretary-General Boutros Boutros-Ghali drew attention to these contradictory movements.

> We have entered a time of global transition. . . . Regional and continental associations of States are evolving ways to deepen cooperation and ease some of the contentious characteristics of sovereign and nationalistic rivalries. National boundaries are blurred by advanced communications and global commerce, and by the decisions of States to yield some sovereign prerogatives to larger, common political associations. At the same time, however, fierce new assertions of nationalism and sovereignty spring up, and the cohesion of States is threatened by brutal ethnic, religious, social, cultural or linguistic strife. Social peace is challenged on the one hand by new assertions of discrimination and exclusion and, on the other, by acts of terrorism seeking to undermine evolution and change through democratic means.[1]

These contrasting developments suggest that, in the new world order, those who have been oppressed by the concentrated power of a centralized system within an acutely divided nation-state will assert the need for

---

1. Boutros Boutros-Ghali, *An Agenda for Peace: Preventive Diplomacy, Peacemaking and Peacekeeping*, A/47/277, S/2411 (United Nations, June 1992), p. 3.

self-determination, while those already free and assured of a cohesive national identity and equitable treatment will modify sovereignty and move toward larger cooperative frameworks.

Nowhere is the tension between the impulses toward unity and autonomy as high as it is in Africa, where the colonial borders have been perceived as both artificial and sacrosanct. Developments in the former Soviet Union, Yugoslavia, Czechoslovakia, and Ethiopia show that old assumptions about borders and nationhood are being reconsidered. Ethiopia, which appears ready to give its ethnic groups the right of self-determination, may well prove a test case on how far Africa will go in reconsidering state borders. There is a widely shared fear in Africa and elsewhere that reconsidering the policy of preserving colonial borders could open a Pandora's box of conflict and threaten the unity of many countries. Disregarding genuine cases for self-determination, however, would be equally dangerous. And it is not certain that making justified exceptions to the preservation of colonial borders would lead to the disintegration of African states. Quite the contrary, it is often argued that African nations have succeeded so well in consolidating most state borders that justified exceptions can now be afforded.

What is critical to appreciate is that the tensions about the breakdown of national borders are a symptom of the contradictions within those borders expressed in sharp disparities. The gross inequities in such countries as Ethiopia and the Sudan must be addressed if the territorial integrity of those countries is to be preserved. Internal displacement is the outcome of conflicts resulting from those contradictions; they need to be understood in the context of the post–cold war world order and the challenges it presents for the United Nations and the international community in meeting humanitarian needs within state borders and promoting the resolution of internal conflicts.

The Tension between Marginalization and Self-Reliance

During the cold war, debate on conflicts around the world, but especially in Africa, focused on whether they were internally rooted or provoked by the ideological and strategic rivalry between the superpowers. The question was crucial to how those conflicts were to be addressed. If the causes were internal, remedies had to be sought internally. If the conflicts were the result of rivalry between the superpowers, the solutions had to be sought through them. Superpower solutions, however, did not depend on who was right or wrong but on who was an ally. From the African perspective, the debate polarized those who welcomed external intervention as necessary and those who resisted it as a complication and aggravation of internal or regional conflicts.[2]

Now that the cold war has ended, the strategies of the major powers are far less concerned with the third world, confirming fears of Africans that the end of the bipolar confrontation would result in the marginalization of the less developed countries. African problems now exist in regional and national but not international contexts. Causes and effects of conflicts are increasingly recognized as primarily internal, a development that has both positive and negative implications.

In the past, Africa was connected to global structures and processes, first by colonial intervention and then by cold war strategies. Having lost those ties, self-reliance in resolving conflicts and encouraging economic development is increasingly imperative. However, having been cut off by their colonial past from the indigenous values and institutions that permit building from within, Africans are left hanging between the local and the global systems. World interest in Africa seems limited to developments in South Africa and the drought-stricken and war-ravaged countries in desperate need of humanitarian assistance. Africans are reacting to what is popularly perceived as marginalization in a pragmatic way that points at two seemingly contradictory but in fact complementary lines of action. They are recognizing that if the world does not care much about them, they must take their destinies into their own hands. At the same time, the imperatives of global interdependence propel them to resist marginalization. Their aim is to put their houses in order through regional resolution of conflicts and improved economic performance, then return to participating in international affairs with a renewed sense of political and economic legitimacy.

These reactions are not sequential but concurrent. Recent years have witnessed a wave of earnest self-criticism in Africa among intellectuals and even incumbent political leaders. Promoting democracy and human

2. For more on this debate, see Francis M. Deng and I. William Zartman, eds., *Conflict Resolution in Africa* (Brookings, 1990).

rights has become a high priority. The Organization of African Unity Charter on Human and Peoples' Rights, the so-called Banjul Charter, was a symbolic step in this effort.[3] And the Conference on Security, Stability, Development, and Cooperation in Africa (CSSDCA), Africa's so-called Helsinki process, which was initiated by General Olusegun Obasanjo's African Leadership Forum and endorsed by the Kampala Conference in Uganda in 1991, is now under consideration by the OAU. It envisages creating an African council of elders, mostly former heads of state and government who have retired respectably and can continue to offer leadership—primarily mediating between parties to domestic and regional conflicts.

OAU Secretary-General Salim A. Salim has also reactivated the Commission on Mediation, Arbitration, and Conciliation and has recently established a conflict resolution unit in the Secretariat. The secretary-general's proposals for conflict prevention and resolution are far-reaching. As he stated in his June 1992 report,

> in the absence of relevant provisions in the Charter, what is needed is a Declaration of the Assembly of Heads of State and Government providing clear terms of reference for the Secretary-General and the Bureau. In that way, a clear basis for their "intervention" would be furnished. Such a Declaration should also provide that the decisions of the Bureau of the Summit should be binding and, thus, enforceable vis-à-vis all Member States. In that way, the apparent shift in the thinking of Member States on the non-interference principle will move from the realm of mere theory to actual practice. The adoption of such a Declaration would be a much-needed stop-gap measure until the more exhaustive process of Charter Review is undertaken to allow for the formal incorporation of its content into the Charter. These would include provisions on the enhanced role of the Secretary-General, the respective roles of the Bureau of the Summit and of the Defence Commission, as well as on the new content of the non-interference principle. Eventually, a Charter Review process would also allow for

---

3. *African Charter on Human and Peoples' Rights*, CAB/LEG/67/3 (Addis Ababa: Organization of African Unity, 1982).

the definitive pronouncement by Member States on the future of the Commission on Mediation, Conciliation and Arbitration.[4]

If these moves can succeed, Africa will be in a better position to resist marginalization. Indeed, Secretary-General Salim has implored Africa to take the lead in building on its traditional values of communal solidarity to transcend conventional notions of sovereignty and promote peaceful resolution of conflicts and cooperation in addressing humanitarian challenges.

The Challenges of the New Order

African problems, whether in conflict management or socioeconomic development, must be approached from knowledge of their local, regional, and national contexts. As in most matters pertaining to Africa, the premise for analyzing modern conditions is the colonial nation-state, which brought together diverse groups that it then kept separate and unintegrated. Regional ethnic groups were broken up and affiliated with others within the artificial borders of the new states; colonial masters imposed a superstructure of law and order to maintain relative peace and tranquility.

The independence movement was a common cause that reinforced the idea of unity within the artificial framework of the newly established nation-state. Initially, independence came as a collective gain that did not disaggregate who was to get what from the legacy of centralized power and wealth. But colonial institutions had divested the local communities and ethnic groups of much of their indigenous autonomy and sustainable livelihood and replaced them with centralized authority and dependency on the welfare state. Once control of these institutions was passed to the nationals at independence, the struggle for central control became unavoidable. The outcome was often conflict—over power, wealth, and opportunities for development—that led to gross violations of human rights, denial of civil liberties, disruption of economic and social life, and consequent frustration of development.[5]

4. *Report of the Secretary-General on Conflicts in Africa: Proposals for an OAU Mechanism for Conflict Prevention and Resolution*, CM/1710 (L.VI) (New York, June 1992), p. 13.

5. Saadia Touval, *The Boundary Politics of Independent Africa* (Harvard University Press, 1972); and Deng and Zartman, *Conflict Resolution in Africa*.

As the cold war raged, however, these conflicts were seen not as domestic struggles for power and resources but as extensions of the superpower ideological confrontation. Rather than help resolve them peacefully, the superpowers often made them worse by providing military and economic aid to their allies.[6] Although the end of the cold war has removed this aggravating external factor, it has also removed the moderating role of the superpowers, both as third parties and mutually neutralizing allies. "Superpower disengagement from Cold War stakes has removed a vital element of coherence," one scholar has written. "Old taboos about offending friends and partners in the developing world—all part of the Cold War dating game—are gone."[7] As events in Liberia, Somalia, and the Sudan illustrate, the results have too often been unmitigated brutalities and devastations.

What occurred in Africa is comparable to what has happened in the countries of the former Soviet Union and Eastern Europe, where a superstructure of authority and control maintained a system of law and order that suppressed the aspirations of nationalities, ethnic groups, and other identities. Although the basic material needs of the population were provided by the state, massive violations or denials of fundamental political and civil rights eventually generated democratic movements that contributed to the collapse of the systems.

The gist of the new internal conflicts is that the ethnic pieces put together by colonial glue and reinforced by the old world order are now pulling apart and reasserting their autonomy. Old identities, rendered dormant by the structures and values of the nation-state system, are reemerging and redefining the standards of political participation, distribution of goods and services, and government legitimacy.

Cultural self-assertions are part of this process. From the dawn of African independence, such slogans as Senghor's "negritude," Nkrumah's "consciencism," Kenyatta's "Uhuru," Nyerere's "Ujamaa," Mobutu's "authenticity," and Kaunda's "humanism" have symbolized

6. Marina Ottaway, "Superpower Competition and Regional Conflicts in the Horn of Africa," in Craig Nation and Mark V. Kauppi, eds., *The Soviet Impact in Africa* (Lexington, Mass.: Lexington Books, 1984), p. 175; Terrence Lyons, "The United States and Ethiopia: The Politics of a Patron-Client Relationship," *Northeast African Studies*, vol. 8, no. 2 (1986), pp. 53–75; and Jeffrey A. Lefebvre, *Arms for the Horn: U.S. Security Policy in Ethiopia and Somalia, 1953–1991* (University of Pittsburgh Press, 1991).

7. Chester A. Crocker, "The Global Law and Order Deficit: Is the West Ready to Police the World's Bad Neighborhood?" *Washington Post*, December 20, 1992, p. C1.

African leaders' search for cultural legitimation of their political and economic strategies. Often the slogans were rationalizations for ideas and practices adopted from foreign prototypes and dressed up in local garb, but they nonetheless expressed a genuine yearning for building on the culture of the people. This yearning is gathering strength. Endowed with a sense of the real world that mere slogans can no longer manage, Africans are now challenged to find workable solutions to real problems—and in the framework of the new world order. As the case of the Sudan shows, it is in this context that Islamic revival in North Africa and the Middle East should be understood.

These complexities, however, do not invalidate the quest for cultural legitimization and the need to undertake nation building and development based on indigenous African values and institutions. The search for workable formulas must consider the conflicting demands for autonomy and equitable unity being made by various groups within a nation-state. The principles must be autonomy, equity, and justice. But the observance of these principles requires a third party as mediator, moderator, peacemaker, and lawgiver. Although regional organizations can participate, the most obvious institution to play a pivotal role is the United Nations, whose global legitimacy has been reinvigorated by the end of the cold war. As Secretary-General Boutros Boutros-Ghali noted, "a conviction has grown, among nations large and small, that an opportunity has been regained to achieve the great objectives of the Charter—a United Nations capable of maintaining international peace and security, of securing justice and human rights and of promoting, in the words of the Charter, 'social progress and better standards of life in larger freedom.' This opportunity must not be squandered. The Organization must never again be crippled as it was in the era that has now passed."[8]

It must be admitted that once the colonial powers accomplished the brutal task of conquest and pacification, they established a system of public order and justice that brought peace to interethnic relations that had been afflicted by chronic violence throughout recorded history. Although colonial intervention understandably provoked nationalistic reactions that ultimately culminated in the independence movement, the postulated role for the United Nations—establishing peace, justice, stability, and prosperity—has a compelling and disarming justification be-

8. Boutros-Ghali, *Agenda for Peace*, p. 2.

cause it represents universal values and not the nationalistic interests of any one country. A political, economic, social, and cultural system that autonomously uses local resources and resourcefulness within the framework of regional and global interdependence can be designed to reconcile the lofty ideals of unity with the imperatives of cultural fragmentation. As units of participation and social orientation, the family, the clan, and the tribe can indeed be complementary rather than antagonistic to the nation and the global order.

The United Nations in the New Order

Before the Persian Gulf war, the West perceived the United Nations as a third-world club and a forum for bashing the wealthier countries, particularly the United States. The war and its aftermath turned the organization, in the perception of the third world, into a Western, specifically U.S., instrument for global operations. Nevertheless, it is widely agreed that with the stewardship of Secretary-General Boutros Boutros-Ghali the United Nations is asserting its leadership more than was possible under the constraints of cold war politics. The new reality is a balance between the collectivism of a UN organization with limited resources and the pivotal role of the powerful Western democracies with effective means for implementing UN decisions. This has clearly established a leadership role for the West.

The United States, or more appropriately former President George Bush, did not shy away from the role of leadership that the new perception of the United Nations places on the West. Despite many member states' resentment of a UN system that has hitherto paid lip service to the principle of equality among members, the real test of whether this leadership is deserved will depend on the extent to which the United States lives up to the ideals of political, economic, and moral leadership, whether it operates on its own or through international institutions.

Although states are usually assumed to be motivated by national interests, the role of a world leader carries with it burdens that should transcend those interests. There is obviously considerable controversy in the United States about what President Bush meant by a new world order, what responsibilities he envisioned for U.S. leadership in that order, and what the financial costs will be. Americans do not seem to have accepted the leadership postulated by Bush, especially if it means greater U.S. expenditures. But the vision clearly remains a controversial issue. When that controversy is resolved, the United States will have to be more specific about what the new order means, whether and how the country will assume leadership, what the guiding principles of leadership will be, and how leadership will act in the various regions where international action is needed to address urgent issues. Somalia has already imposed itself on the international agenda and the former Yugoslavia is competing for attention, but there are many more candidates, and the ultimate objective should be a comprehensively peaceful, just, and orderly world.

If progress is assumed to be an integral part of human development, then the emerging new world order must signify an improvement on the way things have been. This order must recognize and attempt to reconcile seemingly contradictory trends, the quest for autonomy and the need for broadening circles of cooperation regionally and internationally. Leadership at the international level must pursue the ideals of freedom, democracy, justice, and prosperity for all nations and peoples. World leaders must provide protection and assistance to the needy wherever they are; they cannot discriminate between their own nationals and the marginalized nationals of foreign nations, at least not to the extent of dispossession, denial of protection, and deprivation of basic needs. The liberation of a Kuwait or the reconstruction of a Somalia must be defended only on universal principles, not on limited national strategic objectives, if the role of the United States as the driving force behind UN action is to be viewed as global leadership. The same principle is more glaringly necessary in protecting the Kurds in Iraq and imposes an obligation on the United States and the United Nations to exercise the same responsibility in comparable situations needing international action.

As events in Somalia illustrate, action cannot be left to local factions when the extent of human suffering and destruction of life and property far exceeds what should be tolerable even by minimum standards of human dignity and global responsibility. If the international community does not extend the logic of action in Somalia to other areas of massive suffering, we may witness a new world disorder. Nearly a century ago, in 1884–85, the major European powers with the United States in attendance met in Berlin and carved the African continent into pieces of real estate over which they extended colonial dominion. Since independence, Africa's commitment to the preservation of the colonial borders has had the mixed result of keeping the borders stable but generating internal strife and civil wars that have inflicted much suffering on masses of the people. Perhaps the time has come for another Berlin conference, at least a metaphorical one, with a different venue, participants, and guiding principles to examine closely the effect of the decisions taken nearly a century ago on the continent.

It was noted earlier that African conflicts are generated by the diversities and disparities within the rigid borders of the colonial state. It was also noted that in the view of some, African borders have been so stable that states can now permit making exceptions to the rigid rule of preserving the colonial borders. Others fear that this would threaten most states in Africa with disintegration. But rethinking borders does not necessarily imply dismantling existing ones. As the UN secretary-general has noted, "The United Nations has not closed its doors. Yet if every ethnic, religious or linguistic group claimed statehood, there would be no limit to fragmentation, and peace, security and economic well-being for all would become ever more difficult to achieve."[9] What is required is a comprehensive strategy for addressing realistically the problems that threaten national borders from within. Only if it proves impossible to find workable solutions to preserve unity can the revision of borders be justified. But when that conclusion is reached, preserving colonial borders should no longer be regarded as an untouchable; nations should be seen as tools for promoting the security, integrity, and dignity of their citizens. If we are to rethink the colonial borders to give greater meaning to self-determination and the principles of democracy and human dignity, policy analysts must begin to clear the way in what is now a tangled thicket of imposed unity that lacks the necessary foundations for sustaining real unity peacefully and equitably.

International concern with the fundamental human rights of people displaced within their national borders need not conflict with the principle of sovereignty. No government can legitimately invoke sovereignty for the deliberate purpose of starving its population or otherwise denying them protection and resources vital to their survival and well-being. The presumption that if a government is incapable of providing protection and assistance, the international community, either on the invitation of the host country or with international consensus, should act in consonance with the principle of sovereignty.

9. Boutros-Ghali, *Agenda for Peace*, p. 5.

Changing patterns that favor international action are reflected in the recent approaches of the human rights policymaking bodies, which have increasingly resorted to appointing special rapporteurs, working groups, or representatives with mandates relating to sensitive and complex matters of human rights protection and assistance to persons under state jurisdiction. These procedures involve scrutinizing state performance in a way that contrasts with those followed by the United Nations in the past when confidential communications with the states were the only means of addressing human rights issues. The new procedures therefore signify considerable progress on behalf of universal humanitarian assistance and human rights protection.

Judging from the evidence in the countries I visited in connection with the UN mandate, these new trends have clearly transmitted a message of global concern to the masses of the internally displaced. Their aspirations for international protection and assistance have been commensurately lifted. The sense of optimism and empowerment that is emerging is also fostering cooperation from governments and other authorities. The prospects of international cooperation, diplomatic persuasion, and, in exceptional circumstances, collective international action all interact to promote greater attention to the rights and needs of the affected population.

The increasing concern of the international community with the cause of internally displaced persons should not, however, be exaggerated as having adequately met the challenge posed by the humanitarian and human rights agenda for their protection and assistance. Indeed, one of the most significant observations I made in the countries I visited was that aspirations and expectations far exceed the capacity of the UN bodies to deliver the protection and assistance their visibility promises. The challenge is, of course, not to diminish the visibility but to address what Chester Crocker, former U.S. assistant secretary of state for Africa, called the "global law and order deficit," with the view to improve the capacity of the United Nations to respond and deliver.[10]

10. Crocker, "Global Law and Order Deficit," p. C1.

8

The International Response to Civil Violence

When the breakdown of civil society or the outbreak of unmanageable civil violence necessitates a humanitarian intervention from the international community, the precise objectives and conduct of the intervention come under careful scrutiny. Usually, the immediate necessity to deliver relief supplies is compelling and overwhelming. Little attention is paid to the conditions leading to the crisis. But understanding those conditions is critical to the longer-term reconstruction and normalization of a self-sustaining order. Thus the problem is not limited to managing short-term crises or embarking on longer-term solutions. It begins with the question of whether the deterioration of a particular situation merits international intervention, how that intervention is to be conducted, and what its objectives should be.

The Quest for an Intervention Strategy

International responses to internal conflicts and communal violence that threaten civil order should address the challenges in three phases: monitoring developments to draw early attention to impending crises, interceding through diplomatic initiatives in time to avert crises, and mobilizing international active intervention when necessary. A comprehensive strategy of the third phase, intervention, would itself require three phases: arresting the immediate crisis, appraising the causes of the situation, and, if necessary, designing a plan to reconstruct the society and the country.

The outline of a system of international response to conflicts and attendant displacement was provided by UN Secretary-General Boutros Boutros-Ghali in *An Agenda for Peace*. Referring to the end of the cold war and the new demands on the UN Security Council to prevent and resolve conflicts and preserve peace, he wrote:

> Our aims must be: To seek to identify at the earliest possible stage situations that could produce conflict, and to try through diplomacy to remove the sources of danger before violence results;
>
> Where conflict erupts, to engage in peacemaking aimed at resolving the issues that have led to conflict;
>
> Through peacekeeping, to work to preserve peace, however fragile, where fighting has been halted and to assist in implementing agreements achieved by the peacemakers;
>
> To stand ready to assist in peace-building in its differing contexts: rebuilding the institutions and infrastructures of nations torn by civil war and strife; and building bonds of peaceful mutual benefit among nations formerly at war;
>
> And in the largest sense, to address the deepest causes of conflict: economic despair, social injustice and political oppression. It is possible to discern an increasingly common moral perception that spans the world's nations and peoples, and which is finding expression in international laws, many owing their genesis to the work of this Organization.[1]

The secretary-general's enumeration of these principles addresses "the global law-and-order deficit" that former U.S. Assistant Secretary of State for African Affairs Chester Crocker has discussed:

> We need first . . . to understand why regional disorder in Somalia and elsewhere is flourishing and why U.S. leadership in these revolutionary times is vital to our national interests. The short answer is that historic changes since 1989 have profoundly destabilized the previously existing order without replacing it with any recognizable or legitimate system. New vacuums are setting off new conflicts. Old

---

1. Boutros Boutros-Ghali, *An Agenda for Peace: Preventive Diplomacy, Peacemaking and Peacekeeping* (United Nations, June 1992), p. 4.

problems are being solved, begetting new ones. The result of this process is a global law-and-order deficit that is straining the capacity of existing and emerging security institutions.[2]

The requirements of peace accords and the disintegration of governments that no longer enjoy the legitimacy and domestic or external support to survive have placed new demands on the United Nations to deploy peacekeepers, cease-fire observers, election monitors, and even civilian administrators. "Democracy and free markets," Crocker notes, "are not capable of being 'exported' by Voice of America broadcasts or 'taught' through exchanges of scholars. They cannot be imposed by isolation and sanctions."

Thus the international community needs principles for meeting the challenges of the law-and-order deficit:

we do need to address the mounting lack of consensus on basic norms of global political life combined with the shortage of legitimate institutions for handling the resulting security problems. We also need to remedy the scarcity of means for "enforcing" whatever solutions may be agreed upon. Not since the Napoleonic upheavals (if not the Peace of Westphalia in 1648) have the rights of states, people and governments been so unclear.

Under what circumstances are territorial borders to be considered sacrosanct and who shall determine the answer? When do "identity groups" (peoples or ethnic fragments) have the right of secession, autonomy or independence? What "sovereign" rights, if any, do governments have to prevent outsiders from telling them how to treat their people, their economies and their environment? And what about the rights of outsiders to come to the aid of peoples victimized by the actions or inactions of local governments—or to create the functional equivalent of government where, as in Somalia, none exists?

"The law-and-order deficit," Crocker concludes, "cannot be eliminated by relying solely on ad hoc, unilateral U.S. actions, no matter how forceful the decisions or masterful the execution. We urgently need

2. Chester A. Crocker, "The Global Law and Order Deficit: Is the West Ready to Police the World's Bad Neighborhoods?" *Washington Post*, December 20, 1992, p. C1.

some internationally agreed-upon rules and criteria as well as dedicated mechanisms for planning and conducting the internationally sanctioned uses of force."[3]

Concern about the lack of normative principles and enforcement mechanisms for international response to the humanitarian challenges of civil disorder has been widespread. Among the most pertinent questions raised in a Brookings Institution memorandum are how to determine the extent of violence that would justify military intervention to permit the delivery of emergency supplies, what operational designs are appropriate for military action, and what precise objectives intervention should encompass—in particular, whether it should be limited to emergency assistance or extended to the reconstruction of a sustainable civil order (see appendix C). The memorandum emphasizes the inadequacy of international preparedness: indeed, established policies—ineffective sanctions and control of arms flows—inadvertently reinforce violent disintegration, and industrial democracies that would have to fashion an effective response have been unable to form a consensus. There is nonetheless a strong presumption that these democracies cannot operate without defending standards of human rights and political procedures. They could not themselves prosper in a faltering international economy of large contiguous populations; they would descend into endemic violence and economic depression. But the combination of a compelling need to act and a lack of planning for responses makes the United States and Western European countries particularly prone to crisis-induced reactions that are relatively easy to execute but are more symbolic than effective.

International intervention must then, according to the memo, first establish basic civil order under conditions where it has broken down and is unlikely to be regenerated within a reasonable time or at tolerable cost in materiel and human lives. Because such intervention is a major intrusion, resistance on grounds of national sovereignty or pride is a certainty, although there will always be elements in the country who will welcome intervention, especially among the disadvantaged groups it promises to benefit. The justification for intervention must therefore be persuasive, if not beyond reproach: "The difference between an intervention that succeeds and one that is destroyed by immune reaction

3. Crocker, "Global Law and Order Deficit," p. C1.

would depend on the degree of spontaneous acceptance or rejection by the local population."

To avoid or minimize this immune reaction, intervention would have to be broadly international. The principles on which it is based and its objectives must transcend political and cultural boundaries or traditions and concomitant nationalist sentiments. The rationale that could conceivably carry such a burden involves human rights so fundamental—food, clothing, shelter, physical protection, basic health services, and family integrity—that they are not derived from any particular political or economic ideology. Thus there must be a new standard for organizing international relationships. "Any government that fails to provide the most fundamental rights for major segments of its population can be said to have forfeited sovereignty, and the international community can be said to have a duty in those instances to reestablish it. If the absence of functional sovereignty is declared in any situation, assertive measures to recreate it would be allowed."

Although there are a number of practical problems with stating the precise human rights standards to be applied, determining the procedures for declaring the loss of sovereignty, and deciding how to contain gross violations of fundamental rights, a standard must be developed. And as important as the principle that would justify intervention is the design for carrying it out. The memo suggests that in a country with a functional absence of sovereignty, the traditional strategic operations to deter, intimidate, or attack "a coherently managed opponent" would not be effective. In Bosnia and Somalia, for example, the fighting forces are under a command discipline too loose to be effectively controlled by any central leadership. To establish civil order, the intervention would have to disarm and disband the militias or at least deprive them of armed vehicles and heavy weapons.

Disarming militias and maintaining standard civil law in support of relief operations would be the basic military mission of an intervention force. But it would have to be accompanied by reconstitution of a valid government. Thus the memo proposes a two-phase operation. The first would have to be short: a pacification campaign that does not succeed quickly would probably not succeed at all. The required force would need sufficient personnel, firepower, mobility, and information resources to begin decisive combat action. It would also need the command sophistication and operational discipline to fight judiciously:

rather than destroy every marauding band, it would defeat a few in order to intimidate those inclined to resist and reassure those inclined to accommodate. The second phase would aim at keeping basic order in the aftermath of pacification. This would entail reestablishing a functioning political and economic system, which means this phase could take a long time and participating parties would worry about an indefinite commitment.

Most of the memorandum accords with the policy analysis in this study. And although the concept of a functional absence of sovereignty is bound to be controversial and difficult to determine, even the official circles of the United Nations would not find it too radical to entertain. As the secretary-general of the United Nations has observed, "The time of absolute and exclusive sovereignty . . . has passed," and the leaders of states must "find a balance between the needs of good internal governance and the requirements of an ever more interdependent world."[4] Although the secretary-general emphasizes respect for the sovereignty and integrity of the state as crucial to the international system, the transcendent importance of human rights, especially where order has broken down or the state is unable or unwilling to protect the masses of citizens, would make international inaction indefensible.

But the perspectives of the pivotal participants on such matters as the national or public interest are bound to be sharply divided both internally and in their relationship to the outside world. After all, internal conflicts often entail a contest for national power and therefore sovereignty. Every outside political intervention has its internal beneficiaries. Under those circumstances, there can hardly be said to be an indivisible quantum of national sovereignty behind which the nation stands united. Furthermore, it is not always easy to determine how much the government of a country devastated by civil war is truly in control, when, as is often the case, sizable portions of the territory are controlled by opposing forces. Oftentimes, a government may remain in effective control of the capital and the main garrisons, but the economy and social structure of much of the countryside will have practically collapsed. How would such partial but significant collapse be considered in determining the degree to which civil order in the country has broken down?

4. Boutros-Ghali, *Agenda for Peace*, p. 5.

A historical perspective may help refine this question. Sovereignty cannot be a value-free property of whoever claims to represent the country. Initially, it was the prerogative of the crown, which was supreme and above the law. The evolution of democratic values and institutions gradually devolved sovereign will and authority to the people. It is the will of the people, democratically invested in elected leaders, that entitles authorities to uphold the sovereignty of a nation. Where governments fail to meet their fundamental obligations to the whole population or significant parts of it, the people are justifiably entitled to withdraw the trust they have placed in the authorities. Failure to meet obligations is often abundantly clear. No government that will allow hundreds of thousands to starve to death when food can be made available to them, allow them to be exposed to deadly elements when they could be provided with shelter, or allow them to be indiscriminately tortured, brutalized, and murdered by opposing forces can maintain a clear justification to keep the outside world from stepping in to offer protection and assistance in the name of sovereignty.

The High-level Group convened by the InterAction Council of Former Heads of State and Government on January 21, 1993, on the theme "Bringing Africa Back into the Mainstream of the International System" (see appendix D) has considered the question. As the group saw it, the main questions the international community must address include "what degree of humanitarian suffering under what conditions should justify what form of international action, by whom, through what operational mechanisms, and with what precise objectives?"

This means clarifying the principles, the organizational framework, the operational doctrine, and the precise goals of such intervention.

The clarification of the principles would provide guidelines or standards on what would trigger and justify intervention. The organizational framework raises questions as to who would initiate the decision making process for intervention, and once approved, who would conduct the operations. The issue of operations itself raises questions on the military or civilian forces to be used and their preparedness or training for the task. The issue of objectives raises the question of whether the operations should stop at meeting the short-term emergency needs or extend to addressing the causes of the crisis in order to reconstitute a self-sustaining system of public or civil order.[5]

These considerations make it important to monitor developments to determine the appropriate stage for intervention, how to conduct the process in a particular context, what material, human, and cultural resources there are to work with, and what outcome of the intervention should be postulated.

The UN Security Council has endorsed many of the same conclusions. The council has noted with concern "the incidents of humanitarian crises, including mass displacements of population becoming or aggravating threats to international peace and security." It has expressed the belief "that humanitarian assistance should help establish the basis for enhanced stability through rehabilitation and development" and "noted the importance of adequate planning in the provision of humanitarian assistance in order to improve prospects for rapid improvement of the humanitarian situation."[6] This will of course require planning for the phase beyond the immediate emergency.

Beyond the Immediate Emergency

The gap in the two-phase scheme proposed in the Brookings memorandum is that it seems to call for an international rescue operation only after large numbers of people have been victimized and when protection and assistance would bring only a partial salvation for the survivors. A better model for an effective global system of governance would monitor such developments closely, detect trends that threaten disaster, and authorize a timely action that would avert a crisis.

Once a situation has reached a point that calls for intervention, the two-phase design would also need to be more precise in its plans for reconstructing a functional system of civil order. In Somalia, for example, phase one of Operation Restore Hope is almost over.[7] But although

5. "Bringing Africa Back to the Mainstream of the International System, Report on the Conclusions and Recommendations by a High-Level Group, Cape Town, South Africa," New York: InterAction Council, January 1993, para. 62.

6. Note by the president of the Security Council, S/25344, February 26, 1993, p. 1.

7. The Brookings memorandum, it should be noted, was drafted before Operation Restore Hope began.

the phase-two military aspects of keeping basic order after the pacification campaign have already begun, the longer-term task of reconstituting a functioning civil order remains a major challenge whose prospects of success are still unknown.

The memorandum's postulated two phases, focusing on the crisis point as manifested in the breakdown of civil order, correspond to phase three of the strategy for international response postulated in this study, which would involve mobilizing the international community to undertake a rescue operation. The memorandum's second phase, which entails keeping basic order in the aftermath of pacification is essentially an aspect of my third phase—reconstruction and reconstitution of a functioning and self-regenerating system of civil order. A strategy to achieve this broader objective would require a close understanding of the conditions leading to the crisis. Knowing the evolution of the crisis of governance and the interplay of the policies and responses of the various actors—local, regional, and international—becomes a necessary guide for designing appropriate remedies. An international action triggered by an intolerable deterioration in the situation thus becomes both the end of the three-phase strategy aimed at arresting the crisis and the beginning of a more ambitious process of reconstructing and consolidating peace.

Just as my postulated strategy of international response involves three phases so the third phase, restoring and invigorating a self-sustaining system in a strife-torn country, itself requires three phases. The first phase would involve gathering information to determine how the past explains the present. In the second phase the appropriate measures to be taken in the light of the findings would be designed. The third phase would put the strategies into operation. And just as the three phases of the initial response to the crisis are closely intertwined, so would be the phases of rebuilding. Indeed, because the pressures of involvement may be considerable, these rebuilding phases may require simultaneous gathering and processing of information, designing appropriate strategies, and applying the strategies in a flexible way that can continue to respond to new information and adjustments.

In this conceptual framework, appropriate policy analysis of conditions and design of strategies is crucial. Even with the minimum level of international and operational innovations, the strategies for international response would require the United Nations and the international community to make available adequate amounts of resources for the work to provide what it promises. But, at least at the intellectual level, a great deal may depend on the manner in which the potential concern of the international community is used. If my limited personal experience can be illuminating, the pro bono contributions I received from universities, nongovernmental organizations, and a wide array of government and private sources of expertise in preparing my study for the United Nations clearly demonstrates that there is a rich reserve of good will eager to be mobilized for a worthy humanitarian cause. And because what is needed far exceeds what can be generated through the established institutions, this potential resource is vitally important.

Among the tasks that could be independently undertaken would be to develop criteria for determining the extent of human rights violations or the scale of human suffering that would move the international community to intervene. Such standards, even if not formally endorsed by governments and rendered as a legally enforceable instrument, could provide a useful guide and a deterrent to governments and other actors. Once prepared, its formal adoption would in itself be a significant part of diplomatic initiatives in and outside the UN system. Such a standard-setting exercise could have a broad policy dimension whose authority would rest more in its orientation toward moral values than in its legal enforceability. The goal, ultimately, would be for the legal and the moral dimensions to converge in an international instrument setting new standards by which governments will be held accountable. Again, although the final standards would bear the official seal of governments, their preparation could be broad-based, involving universities and research institutions, lawyers and policy analysts, scholars and activists—a truly wide network that would benefit from cooperation.

Seizing the Global Opportunity

The situations in the countries I visited indicate that the international system is going through a significant transformation in two respects. One is the emergence of a country's human rights record as a legitimate concern for the international community and a basis for scrutinizing the performance of the government and other domestic actors involved. The other transformation is the concern of the international community with civil wars and other domestic violence that inflict suffering on masses of people, among whom the internally displaced are often the most affected. Together these two concerns are early signs of a new world order in which human dignity for all people will become a matter of cooperative international interest. This offers an opportunity that must be seized.

What makes this change particularly significant is that until recently the subject of human rights was considered so sensitive that it was either ignored or treated gingerly as a matter for confidential communications with the governments concerned. Complaints were received by the appropriate UN bodies and, if found admissible, transmitted to the government involved for comments. It was hoped that bringing the complaints to the attention of the government and asking it to respond would raise its level of awareness and motivate it to remedy the situation. The actual behavior of the government was not monitored to ensure that the desired result was achieved.

Since the end of the cold war, however, the international community has been able to take a closer and more sympathetic look at the internal conditions in a country and the needs of its people. The increased exposure of a country's internal dynamics has allowed a better understanding of the conditions there. As a consequence there has been increased international concern about the conditions of the masses of people trapped and victimized by internal wars and the gross violations of human rights that often follow.

In sharp contrast to its often vague response during the cold war, the United Nations is now closely observing conditions in all the countries I have discussed. In four it has a presence on the ground that is directly related to the internal conflicts, whether to deliver assistance and help in peacemaking, as is the case in Somalia and the former Yugoslavia, or to cooperate with the parties in peacekeeping and promoting human rights, as in El Salvador and Cambodia. And in sharp contrast to the cold war attitude of the Soviet Union, the Russian Federation is interested in seeing the United Nations assume a greater role in international efforts to provide protection and assistance for the internally displaced.

Of course, the removal of the centralized controls of the old authoritarian regimes has in certain parts of the world resulted in upheavals that have created new problems for both peace and respect for human rights, as conditions in both the former Soviet Union and former Yugoslavia dramatically illustrate. It is not yet clear what consequences the ripple effect of these changes might have on governments. However, the challenge to the international community is to assist in the reconstruction of national constitutional and legal systems based on respect for fundamental rights. With no major strategic or ideological interests creating obstacles to international cooperation, the United Nations now can be more assertive in promoting peace and respect for human rights.

It was perhaps because of the potential role of the United Nations in providing assistance and fostering peace that my visits as the special representative of the secretary-general were well received, not only by the affected populations but also by the authorities. The mere fact that a representative of the secretary-general had arrived in a remote village by plane, helicopter, or motor vehicle with UN identification was a powerful symbol of international concern that both the government and the people took seriously. It signaled that the world is indeed prepared to be of assistance through international cooperation and collective action.

What all this means is that momentum in a global moral imperative is gathering and that world leaders are called upon to transcend national boundaries to meet their moral obligation toward humanity. The moral distinction implicit in the contrasting conditions of the camps for the Serbs and those for Muslims or non-Serbs cannot be justified in a world that now claims greater sensitivity than ever before to the ideals of the Universal Declaration of Human Rights. And if this call to meet moral obligations is directed to all those who see themselves as international leaders because of their global power and authority, it is particularly pertinent to the United Nations as the organization that embraces the whole of humanity. As this role is redefined to meet the emerging global challenges, the United Nations itself will need to be reinvigorated structurally and operationally.

In nearly all the countries where internal conflicts cause mass dislocation and suffering, there is much the international community, specifically the United Nations, can do not only to provide assistance and protection to the affected population but also to help bring durable peace. Nor does the international community have to wait until conditions have deteriorated as badly as in Somalia and the former Yugoslavia before acting decisively. Much preventive action can be taken that would make international involvement far more cost-effective than the massive intervention that crises always require.

9

A Strategy for Protection

The spotlight of international attention has been focused in the past few years on the tragic conditions in Somalia and the former Yugoslavia. And such a focus is appropriate when civil order has collapsed, when gross violations of fundamental human rights and humanitarian tragedies have occurred, and when it is clearly the responsibility of the international community to provide humanitarian protection and assistance and to help restore political and civil order. But serious violations of human rights affect tens of millions of people around the world every year. Indeed, there are currently 25 million internally displaced people alone, and their numbers are certain to grow. So focusing on the worst situations must not obscure the pervasiveness of the problems or the range of cooperative and diplomatic strategies available for dealing with them. To design measures appropriate to individual cases, it is essential to consider both the general and the unique aspects of each case. And legal standards for intervention and mechanisms for implementation should be scrutinized in the context of international norms of sovereignty that account for the extent to which the international system provides or denies protection and assistance to internally displaced persons.

The Challenge in Perspective

Human rights, humanitarian, and refugee law provide the basis for international concern with the problems of the internally displaced. And the United Nations and various international agencies have responded recently to crises in Bosnia, Somalia, and elsewhere involving internally displaced persons. But much of this action has been ad hoc and has tended to emphasize assistance. Protecting human rights has been a subsidiary consideration. The international community is still in the process of formally recognizing the needs of the internally displaced to be protected and has not yet established a mechanism for their protection or a body with specific responsibility for them. Appointing a representative of the secretary-general for the internally displaced was a significant first step, but much more needs to be done to devise standards of protection and ways to enforce them.

Other than the obvious desire to allay human suffering, there are compelling reasons for stating principles and designing mechanisms that would help prevent the collapse of civil order. Conditions in Somalia and the former Yugoslavia, for example, demonstrate that the international community is far less equipped to respond to extreme situations than it is to less acute circumstances. Besides, prevention is simply better than belated intervention. Prevention would also, no doubt, save lives among the forces of crisis intervention and would be far less expensive.

Whether the measures the international community needs to take are to persuade or to coerce governments, principles that justify international protection of the displaced and the operational means for such involvement must be clarified. Clarification would also help prevent crises because it would provide criteria for determining early the severity of human rights violations that would trigger international response.

The challenge posed by internal displacement involves principles of humanitarianism and human rights so basic—physical protection, shelter, food, clothing, basic health care, and the integrity of the person and the family as the most fundamental social unit—that they do not represent political or ideological interests of individual countries or camps. Existing principles of international law require national governments and the international community to guarantee humane treatment and provide these basic necessities.

The responsibility for meeting these needs falls first on national governments. Where governments cannot provide adequate protection and assistance, they may ask the international community for help. Where governments are unwilling to accept international support, the problem can in most cases be resolved through diplomacy. It is only in the most extreme situations that the international community may be compelled to force access and provide protection and assistance.

The measures needed to meet the challenge are both legal and institutional ones. Filling gaps in the coverage of existing humanitarian law must be a longer-term effort. As an immediate measure, however, it is essential to compile relevant international instruments and standards into comprehensive documents focused on the human rights and humanitarian problems of internal displacement. This measure would also lay the foundation for longer-term objectives. Among the documents envisaged would be a statement of guiding principles, a code of conduct, a declaration, and, as an objective to be achieved through an evolutionary process, a convention on the protection of the displaced.

Although the compilation would help foster an appropriate legal climate for assisting displaced persons, the real issue is not so much deficiencies in the law as inadequacies of enforcement procedures and a lack of political will on the part of both the perpetrators of violations and the international community. It is therefore important to establish a comprehensive mechanism in the international system that would address the protection and assistance needs of displaced persons, recognizing that human rights matters intersect with humanitarian, political, and economic considerations.

The UN secretary-general, in his 1992 annual report, said that devising a clear UN approach to the problem of internal displacement would be timely. Although the study that I prepared for the Commission on Human Rights touched on such general considerations, it focused on the work of the commission. The means available to the commission for helping the internally displaced are working groups, rapporteurs, and special representatives, both on specific issues and for individual countries. Assigning the mandate on internally displaced persons to a representative of the secretary-general was widely perceived as an important first step in addressing the complex and delicate political, human rights, and humanitarian issues connected with the problem and the need to use the people and material resources of the UN system.

The commission did, however, have to decide formally whether it should establish a permanent mechanism for protecting the internally displaced and, if so, what form it should take. The consensus was that a mechanism was needed, but as to its form, views ranged from open-minded advocacy of any of the means already available to assumptions that the form chosen by the commission, namely representative of the secretary-general, should serve that purpose well.

More broadly, there was the question of whether to create a special UN agency for the internally displaced. Short of establishing a new agency, the most logical step would be to redefine the mandates of the High Commissioner for Refugees and the Department of Humanitarian Affairs so that they explicitly covered the internally displaced. Another option would be for all UN agencies whose activities bear on the problems of the internally displaced to become even more attentive to their needs. To the degree that addressing these problems requires the cooperation of the entire UN system, many, including the high commissioner for refugees herself, believe that the representative of the secretary-general might be an effective catalyst for mobilizing the various UN agencies. As representative of the secretary-general, I had already found that cooperating with these agencies and forming a working relationship with the under secretary-general for humanitarian affairs and the secretary-general himself gave the mandate a useful profile in the international system. The advantage was demonstrated by the helpful reactions of the authorities and the displaced people in the countries I visited. To a certain extent, therefore, the representative could help the Secretariat and the UN system protect the human rights of the internally displaced.

My study for the United Nations also suggested that the representative might gather an informal task force or, at a minimum, consult with representatives of the specialized agencies and other UN organs to provide a continuing overview of the work of the United Nations pertaining to the internally displaced. This would help detect any protection problems that might occur and seek appropriate ways to address them.

The study also argued that to be comprehensive, a program of protection and assistance would require further action by the commission and other UN bodies. First, whichever mechanism was adopted, events would have to be monitored to detect early signs of displacement. Public reports would then be submitted to the commission, through the secretary-general to the General Assembly, and, at times, the Security Council, which might ultimately authorize collective international actions. To achieve that objective, other initiatives might be necessary to address related interactive issues.

A Call to Action

The purpose of my original study was to evaluate international legal instruments and aid mechanisms to develop a strategy for dealing with internally displaced persons. More specifically, resolution 1992/73 of the Commission on Human Rights mandated the secretary-general to recommend ways to strengthen existing laws and mechanisms to make them more effective in providing protection for the internally displaced (see appendix A).

With respect to the laws, I encountered two perspectives. One was that existing standards sufficiently cover the internally displaced and that the principal problem was lack of implementation. The other was that there were gaps in the coverage of the standards that needed to be filled to make them adequate. Both points of view emanated from the need to strengthen protection for the displaced. The first favored building on what already existed and worried that any arguments about gaps in coverage might weaken the force of existing laws and perhaps even encourage violations, since it might be argued that there was nothing to violate. The second believed that setting new standards would not only fill existing gaps but also focus international attention and thereby increase public awareness of the problem and the need for remedies.

The study found that insofar as the principles were concerned, there indeed appeared to be fairly adequate protection under human rights and humanitarian law. There were, however, obvious gaps in addressing less organized violence within countries and the specific needs of internally displaced persons. It was not sufficient to argue that the displaced, as human beings, are by definition covered by all human rights and humanitarian protection available in the law. Just as added attention and protection were required for minorities, women, children, the disabled, refugees, and other vulnerable groups, a specific regime for protecting the internally displaced would focus on their special needs.

That there are gaps in coverage and a chronic problem of insufficient implementation tends to favor the development of a legal instrument specifically addressing internal displacement. But preparing it will take time. Meanwhile, the urgent needs of the internally displaced called for a speedy remedy. The study recommended that although work might usefully begin on a legal instrument, it would be necessary to move ahead with other means of addressing internal displacement. This transitional phase could produce an initial statement of principles that, though not legally binding, would focus international attention, raise the level of awareness, and stimulate practical measures of alleviating the crisis. It would also prepare the ground for a more legally binding document.

Three documents were envisaged. One would be a compilation of rules and norms that already existed in various forms. Another would be a code of conduct comprising guiding principles to govern the treatment of internally displaced persons. The third would be the closest to an authoritative legal document and could take the form of a declaration. These documents would not need to be prepared consecutively; indeed, it might be advantageous to work on them concurrently.

The study found that there was no one organization in the United Nations specifically mandated to assume responsibility for protecting the internally displaced. But given the global magnitude and urgency of the problem, the United Nations would have to look for solutions. One way would be to add internally displaced persons to the mandates of the High Commissioner for Refugees or the Department of Humanitarian Affairs or to establish an equivalent body. Pending the resolution of this institutional choice, the study suggested that each major organ of the UN system whose mandate was relevant consider establishing a unit to focus on the internally displaced. But protection still would need to be addressed by UN human rights bodies. An effective mechanism established by the Commission on Human Rights would serve the purpose by using existing UN institutional structures and resources.

Such a mechanism might have three principal activities. One would involve monitoring, gathering information, processing it, reporting to pertinent authorities within the system, and issuing bulletins that could act as early warnings of impending displacement crises and call for action against current violations. The second would comprise making contacts with governments and other actors to facilitate dialogue and otherwise seek ways to ameliorate the suffering of the displaced. The third would entail invoking alternative enforcement mechanisms where dialogue failed.

Which of the mechanisms available to the commission—representative of the secretary-general, rapporteur, or working group—would be better able to use the potential of the UN system? Each offered particular advantages, but perhaps a pivotal factor in selecting among them was the need for liaison with other UN bodies, including the General Assembly and, ultimately, the Security Council. As such, the good offices of the secretary-general might be an advantage. This suggested that a representative of the secretary-general might be the best choice. The broad rubric under which the representative would operate would permit creative monitoring, reporting, and otherwise putting in motion early warning systems to reinforce diplomatic initiatives before more drastic measures might be considered.

The principles of the legal doctrine and the institutional mechanism could be put into operation in three phases: monitoring, reporting, and early warning; intercession, dialogue, and mediation; and eventual humanitarian collective action.

Phase one would detect the problem by collecting information, evaluating it, and reporting it. The phase would make use of the UN network, including the early warning system recommended by the Administrative Committee on Coordination that would establish an interagency consultative mechanism. This early warning system would especially benefit from the reports of field representatives and other monitors from the High Commissioner for Refugees, the UN Development Program, UNICEF, and other intergovernmental and nongovernmental bodies, including the Organization of African Unity, the Organization of American States, and other regional groups.

The result of phase one would be to declare the existence of a problem, its magnitude, and the need for measures to resolve it. This statement should precipitate phase two, although enough would already be known to warrant the involvement of the representative of the secretary-general. The simultaneous actions imply some functional overlap. Through missions to a country the representative could also detect developments that might lead to massive displacement and bring them to the attention of the international community. The outcome of the representative's discussions with the relevant government would determine whether action would be needed. The representative might become convinced by the analyses available from phase one or by insights from an initial trip to the country that some sort of humanitarian action was urgently needed. Nevertheless, the representative might choose to continue the dialogue.

If the situation continued to threaten lives, the representative would need to engage other bodies within the United Nations, if necessary through the secretary-general. This is when the principles of the legal doctrine and especially the guiding principles of the code of conduct would help determine the action required. As already indicated, the clarification of those principles could be an important aspect of prevention. The expectation that if specified standards were not met, certain consequences would follow could be an effective deterrent. A standard stipulating that "any government that fails to provide the most fundamental rights for major segments of its population can be said to have forfeited sovereignty, and the international community can be said to have a duty in those instances to reestablish it," could indeed generate a desired response as a country attempted to avoid being declared a legitimate target for humanitarian intervention (see memorandum, appendix C). By the same token the standard, when there was convincing evidence of a country's failure to respond, would sanction mounting an international rescue mission for protecting the dispossessed.

Postscript

The Response of the Commission on Human Rights

The study of human rights issues relating to internally displaced persons from which this book is derived was submitted by the secretary-general of the United Nations for consideration at the forty-ninth session of the Commission on Human Rights in February 1993. After extended discussion, representatives of governments and international organizations voiced overwhelming support for its conclusions and recommendations. Even those who emphasized the complexities of the problem of displacement and the need for caution in approaching it as a human rights issue endorsed the conclusions and recommendations. In this brief review I present some of the responses at the session.

A week before the session commenced, the Norwegian government had hosted a roundtable conference, cosponsored by the Norwegian Refugee Council and the Refugee Policy Group, at Nyon, Switzerland, on the problems of internally displaced persons. The conference helped prepare the ground for a constructive consideration of the internally displaced by the commission. It was the first public forum in which the main themes, conclusions, and recommendations of the study were presented.

Roundtable participants encouraged a greater role for the Commission on Human Rights in the protection of internally displaced persons because the commission, unlike humanitarian bodies, could address the causes of displacement and focus attention on problems of protection.

Participants expressed support for the continuation and expansion of the mandate of the secretary-general's representative and identified gaps that should be filled to increase protection for internally displaced persons.[1] The roundtable recommended that information on serious situations of internal displacement needed to be collected and published so they would not be "forgotten." Information-gathering and fact-finding missions would seek to produce action-oriented reports on an annual or emergency basis. The reports could include case studies of situations in which humanitarian assistance and access were being denied, starvation was being used as a weapon of war, and women and children confronted serious protection problems.

The roundtable also recommended that diplomatic intercessions and dialogue with governments and nongovernmental entities be undertaken to prevent emergencies and produce remedies. The actions needed to be coordinated with humanitarian agencies and regional bodies involved with the internally displaced to ensure that protection problems were addressed. Finally, international action needed to be triggered in serious cases by bringing problems to the attention of governments, the secretary-general, and the Security Council when appropriate. Participants noted that the carrying out of these functions by the representative would be a first step toward creation of a focal point within the UN system for protection of internally displaced persons.[2]

The themes of the roundtable conference were later reflected in the discussions of the commission at its forty-ninth session, which formally considered the study on the internally displaced.[3] Commenting specifically on the study, the delegate from Norway acknowledged the willingness on the part of the governments visited to cooperate as "very encouraging." He suggested that UN action should be based on a "comprehensive approach, bringing together prevention, protection and solutions." The delegate concluded with a recommendation for the continuation of the mandate of the representative of the secretary-general.

1. *Norwegian Government Roundtable Discussion on United Nations Human Rights Protection for Internally Displaced Persons, Held in Nyon, Switzerland* (Washington: Norwegian Refugee Council and UN Refugee Policy Group, February 1993), p. 37.

2. *Norwegian Government Roundtable Discussion*, p. 17.

3. UN Commission on Human Rights, "Responses of Governments and Agencies to the Report of the U.N. Special Representative for Displaced Persons," Geneva, February 25, 1993. This is a photocopied collection of responses on unnumbered pages.

Concurring with one of the study's suggestions for institutional arrangements outside the commission's framework, the Swedish delegate stated that it was important to have a focal point within the UN system for collecting information on the internally displaced. He saw such a focal point as existing in conjunction with and supporting the activities of the representative of the secretary-general. The delegation of Austria, one of the principal movers of resolution 1992/73, which had mandated the representative of the secretary-general, was also a staunch supporter of the study. Like the Norwegian delegate, the Austrian delegation welcomed the representative's invitation from governments experiencing internal displacement and advocated extension of the representative's mandate. Cyprus, one of the countries that had responded substantively to the request for information, called the study "a thorough examination of the different aspects of the problems of displaced persons [that] constitutes an important contribution to determining the legal and policy approaches to be adopted by the United Nations." Hungary credited the study with "properly reflecting the existing situation." It drew attention to the political changes since the end of the cold war that have resulted in the emergence of new sovereign states and made the point that this development should be accompanied by policies that ensure the adherence to international humanitarian law and human rights.

The High Commissioner for Refugees, whose agency is one of the UN organs assisting the internally displaced the most, hoped that the study would result in an "appropriate follow-up mechanism that furthers the development of concrete legal and practical measures to meet the need of displaced persons for protection, humanitarian assistance and solutions." Among the nongovernmental organizations, the Friends (Quakers) World Committee for Consultation, which had been a strong advocate for the commission's involvement in protecting and assisting the internally displaced, also approved extending the representative's mandate.

The delegate from the Sudan, although supporting the conclusions and recommendations of the study, predictably took issue with the analysis of the conflict that underlies the displacement problems in the Sudan and also disagreed with the reports of Africa Watch on the resulting human rights violations. The delegate's statement admitted that "the war in the Southern Sudan together with the drought in the North have resulted in over 3 million Sudanese under this unfortunate category of the internally displaced," and expressed the view that "the International Community is duty bound to extend adequate assistance to the displaced to alleviate their suffering in close collaboration with the governments in question." But he argued that "the question of human rights is only a part of the problem of the internally displaced." On alleged human rights violations, the Sudan expressed "strong reservations on the credibility and authenticity of the obviously exaggerated information quoted in the report based on Africa Watch reports." As for the analysis of the conflict, "the views expressed in the report represented the personal opinion of the author of the report which were publicly known for quite a good time."

The spokesman went on to state that the political aspects of the conflict in southern Sudan, "being an internal issue," do not fall within the mandate of the representative of the secretary-general; that the conflict there is neither religious nor racial; and that all references in the report to the relationship between religion and the state or the ideology of the government also fall outside the scope of the mandate of the representative and are therefore not acceptable. The Sudanese delegate conceded that "the report also contained a number of constructive proposals regarding solutions to the problem of the Sudanese internally displaced. . . . The question however remains . . . whether the International Community in collaboration with the Sudanese government would live up to its obligations and provide assistance in implementing such alternatives and proposals." He commented favorably on the report as a whole.

Sri Lanka and India saw the problem of the internally displaced as having dimensions that went beyond the specific issues of human rights and therefore recommended caution. Sri Lanka argued that "the causes and consequences of displacement had to be approached from other equally valid perspectives." The statement went on to say "given a lack of a definition, a generalized distinction between the protection and assistance needs of the internally displaced and the rest of the civilian population is, in most cases theoretical." Even where the cause is armed conflict or internal strife, the statement continued, the needs of the internally displaced could not be distinguished from those of the people who have not been displaced but whose needs are similar.

Stressing that the causes and consequences of displacement also have to be considered in the context of environmental and socioeconomic factors, Sri Lanka argued that an emphasis only on human rights is limited because it does not usually highlight "terrorist activities" by nonstate factions that often cause internal displacement. What was needed was greater cooperation among the agencies that deliver relief assistance. Sri Lanka, however, supported the representative's suggestion that there be a compilation of existing international standards most relevant to the protection of the rights of the internally displaced.

India's comments were very similar to Sri Lanka's. The Indian delegation welcomed the report of the representative but argued that the "causes and consequences for internal displacement cannot merely be understood from one underlying assumption that all mass movements of persons leading to internal displacement are caused by violation of civil and political rights." In addition to natural disasters, poverty, or lack of development, displacement could also be caused by terrorist activities that do not fall under the work of the commission. The statement suggested that further work on this subject by the commission should be based on the "actual experience of member states [that] have been suffering from internal displacements for a variety of reasons." In support of the concept of sovereignty, India pointed out that "a right to [humanitarian] access over and above the means already available is redundant in a vast majority of cases where states have accepted their moral and legal obligations of providing assistance and protection."

China submitted the most stringent defense of sovereignty while simultaneously stressing that the promotion of human rights and fundamental freedoms is "a lofty goal of mankind." Citing the UN Charter and its insistence that the development of "friendly relations among nations be based . . . on the principle of sovereign equality of all members," China warned against interference in internal affairs of other countries by "the self-interested" concepts of human rights, values, and ideologies of "a few countries."[4]

The Chinese maintained that although the cold war had come to an end and the international situation had undergone significant changes, its vestiges were still affecting the work of the commission. "The practice of distorting human rights standards, exerting political pressure

---

4. Although the statement did not refer to the study on internally displaced persons or the specific issue of a mechanism for their protection and assistance, a Chinese delegate later approached me and said, "We will support the extension of your mandate."

through abuse of monitoring mechanisms, applying selectivity and double standards have led to the violation of principles and purposes of the UN Charter, the impairing of the sovereignty and dignity of many developing countries. Thus the beautiful term of human rights has been tarnished." The statement argued that "any rationalization must have a correct direction and aim" that will reflect the purposes of the UN Charter so as "to develop friendly relations among nations based on respect for the principle of equal rights and self-determination of peoples" and "to achieve international co-operation." It went on to say,

> the urgent issue is to remove as soon as possible . . . the imposition of their own human rights concepts, values and ideology by a few countries who style themselves as "human rights judges" and the interference in internal affairs of other countries by using human rights as a means of applying political pressure. The victims of such practice are developing countries whose people suffered from violation of human rights and fundamental freedoms for a long time before and are now making great efforts to safeguard their sovereignty and independence for their survival and development.

On this issue, the Sudan, whose government's human rights performance was under consideration by the commission, agreed with China. Quoting resolution 1992/39 to the effect "that the promotion, protection and full realization of all human rights and fundamental freedoms should be guided by the principles of nonselectivity and should not be used for political ends" and that "an impartial and fair approach to human rights contributes to the promotion of international cooperation and to the promotion, protection and effective realization of human rights and fundamental freedoms," the delegate of the Sudan asserted that "the politically motivated issues before the current session of the Commission can easily be identified" and alleged that "a number of developing countries were brought under the Commission's concern because of problems relating to bilateral issues." Without elaboration, the statement specified the Sudan as "a country where the United States of America was launching since last year a consistent politically motivated campaign . . . based on a resolution issued by its legislative organs on September 30, 1992." The statement concluded with an ironic suggestion: "This Commission in cooperation with the Centre for Human

Rights should compile an annual report indexing the comparative record of all member states with respect to various defined categories of basic rights. The Human Rights Centre and the Commission should develop a system of rating to measure compliance with each of the basic rights. The delegation of the Sudan is prepared to cooperate in formulating a detailed plan regarding the mechanism and the criteria of this proposal."

The commission adopted resolution 1993/105 on March 11, 1993, without a vote (see appendix B). In its preambular paragraphs, the commission stated that internally displaced persons are in need of relief assistance and protection and expressed its awareness of the "absence of a focal point within the United Nations system to gather information on the situation of internally displaced persons." On the substance of the study, the commission noted that the representative of the secretary-general had identified tasks requiring further study, including the compilation of existing rules and norms and the question of general guiding principles to govern the treatment of internally displaced persons. The commission expressed its appreciation to governments, in particular those that enabled the representative to undertake on-site visits.

On the issue of a special mandate for the internally displaced, the commission requested the secretary-general to instruct his representative to continue for two years the work "aimed at a better understanding of the general problems faced by internally displaced persons and their possible long-term solutions, with a view to identify, where required, ways and means for improved protection for and assistance to internally displaced persons." The commission particularly encouraged the representative to intensify his dialogue with governments and to cooperate and coordinate with the Department of Humanitarian Affairs, the Office of the United Nations High Commissioner for Refugees, and the International Committee of the Red Cross. The representative was requested to submit annual reports on his activities to the Commission on Human Rights and to the General Assembly and "to make any suggestions and recommendations enabling him to better carry out his tasks and activities."

In considering the appropriate course of action by the commission, the sponsors of the resolution tried to strike a balance between supporting the conclusions and recommendations of the study and meeting the concerns governments might have about the sensitive political issues involved. The strategy they chose was to word the resolution in broad terms that would permit flexibility and creativity without exposing details that might generate concern. Because of this care, the study received support as strong and broad as could have been expected under those circumstances.

It is, however, obvious that the challenges posed by internal displacement go beyond what the representative of the secretary-general or indeed the Commission on Human Rights can do within the framework of its well-established special procedures mechanisms. Ultimately, the whole of the UN system and the international community must develop the norms and means for a response commensurate to the challenge. The recommendations in the study aimed at fostering this larger objective are therefore still posited for consideration. As for the three-phase strategy of international response envisaged in the role of the representative, much will depend on how the mandate is in fact carried out: the coordination of activities within the UN system, the cooperation of other actors in the international community, especially the major powers, and the resources made available for these tasks and activities. Ultimately, the United Nations and indeed the international community will have to address the need for an agency for the internally displaced, for expanding the mandate of the High Commissioner for Refugees to formally include the internally displaced, or for establishing within the Secretariat a high-level position to cater to the multifaceted human rights and humanitarian concerns of the internally displaced that are now only partially covered by the mandate of the Department of Humanitarian Affairs. The commission has clearly made a significant beginning; it is now for others within the international system to take the necessary steps toward addressing a worldwide crisis of grave magnitude.

Appendix A

UN Commission on Human Rights Resolution 1992/73

The United Nations Commission on Human Rights,

Mindful of its responsibility under the Charter of the United Nations to promote and encourage respect for human rights and fundamental freedoms,

Recalling the relevant norms of international human rights instruments as well as of international humanitarian law,

Deeply disturbed by the serious problem that the large number of internally displaced persons throughout the world and their suffering is creating for the international community.

Recognizing that internally displaced persons are in need of relief assistance and of protection,

Conscious of the human rights dimensions of internally displaced persons,

Recalling its resolution 1991/25 of 5 March 1991, in which it requested the Secretary-General to submit an analytical report on internally displaced persons, taking into account the protection of human rights of internally displaced persons, based on information submitted by Governments, the specialized agencies, relevant United Nations organizations, regional and intergovernmental organizations, the International Committee of the Red Cross and non-governmental organizations,

1. Takes note of the analytical report of the Secretary-General on internally displaced persons (E/CN.4/1992/23);

2. Requests the Secretary-General to designate a representative to seek to gain views and information from all Governments on the human rights issues related to internally displaced persons, including an examination of existing international human rights, humanitarian and refugee law and standards and their applicability to the protection of and relief assistance to internally displaced persons;

3. Encourages the Secretary-General to seek also views and information from the specialized agencies, relevant United Nations organs, regional intergovernmental and non-governmental organizations and experts in all regions on these issues, as well as of the Emergency Relief Coordinator, the Office of the United nations High Commissioner for Refugees, the International Organization for Migration, the International Committee of the Red Cross and the Ad Hoc Working Group on Early Warning regarding New Flows of Refugees and Displaced Persons established by the Administrative Committee on Coordination;

4. Encourages all interested Governments to make known their views on the subject;

5. Requests the Secretary-General to submit a comprehensive study to the Commission at its forty-ninth session, identifying existing laws and mechanisms for the protection of internally displaced persons, possible additional measures to strengthen implementation of these laws and mechanisms and alternatives for addressing protection needs not adequately covered by existing instruments;

6. Invites the Office of the United Nations High Commissioner for Refugees, the International Organization for Migration and the International Committee of the Red Cross to contribute to the preparation of this study;

7. Decides to continue its consideration of the question at its forty-ninth session under an appropriate agenda item.

Appendix B

UN Commission on Human Rights Resolution 1993/105

The United Nations Commission on Human Rights,

Mindful of its responsibility under the Charter of the United Nations to promote and encourage respect for human rights and fundamental freedoms,

Recalling the relevant norms of international human rights instruments as well as of international humanitarian law,

Deeply Disturbed by the large number of internally displaced persons throughout the world and conscious of the serious problem this is creating for the international community,

Recognizing that internally displaced persons are in need of relief assistance and of protection,

Conscious of the human rights as well as the humanitarian dimensions of internally displaced persons,

Aware of the absence of a focal point within the United Nations system to gather information on the situation of the internally displaced persons and also of the absence of a funding mechanism,

Recalling its resolution 1992/73 of 5 March 1992, in which it requested the Secretary-General to designate a representative to seek to gain views and information from all Governments on the human rights issues related to internally displaced persons, including an examination of existing international human rights, humanitarian and refugee law and standards and their applicability to the protection of and relief assistance to internally displaced persons,

Noting with appreciation the efforts undertaken by the Representative of the Secretary-General to prepare the study, in implementation of his mandate in the short time available to him,

Welcoming the active participation of the Representative of the Secretary-General in the missions of the Special Rapporteur on the situation of human rights in the former Yugoslavia,

Noting that the Representative of the Secretary-General has identified a number of tasks requiring further attention and study including the compilation of existing rules and norms and the question of general guiding principles to govern the treatment of internally displaced persons, in particular their protection and the provision of relief assistance, and also noting his suggestions and recommendations including those relating to vulnerable groups, particularly women and children,

1. Takes note with appreciation of the comprehensive study contained in the annex to the note by the Secretary-General (E/CN.4/1993/35) and of the useful suggestions and recommendations contained therein,

2. Commends the Representative of the Secretary-General for his study and for the way he has started to discharge his mandate,

3. Expresses its appreciation to Governments, in particular those which enabled the Representative to undertake on-site visits, as well as to bodies, programs and organizations of the United Nations system, and to intergovernmental and non-governmental organizations for the cooperation extended to the Representative of the Secretary-General;

4. Requests the Secretary-General to mandate his Representative for a period of two years to continue his work aimed at a better understanding of the general problems faced by internally displaced persons and their possible long-term solutions, with a view to identify, where required, ways and means for improved protection for and assistance to internally displaced persons;

5. Encourages the Representative of the Secretary-General to intensify in this regard his dialogue with governments and to cooperate and coordinate with the Department of Humanitarian Affairs, the Office of the United Nations High Commissioner for Refugees and the International Committee of the Red Cross;

6. Welcomes the cooperation already established between the Representative of the Secretary-General and other United Nations mechanisms and procedures in the field of human rights, and encourages the continuation of this cooperation;

7. Calls upon all governments, regional intergovernmental organizations, the Department for Humanitarian Affairs, the Office of the United Nations high Commissioner for Refugees, the International Organization for Migration, the International Committee of the Red Cross and nongovernmental organizations to continue to cooperate with the Representative and assist him in his tasks and activities;

8. Further calls upon all Governments to continue to facilitate the tasks and activities of the Representative, including, where appropriate, through extending invitations for country visits;

9. Requests the Representative of the Secretary-General to submit annual reports on his activities to the Commission on Human Rights and to the General Assembly and to make any suggestions and recommendations enabling him to better carry out his tasks and activities;

10. Decides to continue consideration of the question of internally displaced persons at its fiftieth session.

Appendix C

Memorandum: Civil Violence as an International Security Problem

As current conditions in Bosnia and in Somalia have demonstrated, the international community has not developed either the principles or the mechanisms for establishing basic civil order in instances where it has collapsed within a sovereign state. Indeed established policies are inadvertently reinforcing violent disintegration. Loose economic sanctions, military detachment and uncontrollable arms flows have this effect.

The problem is everywhere unwelcome and that fact contributes materially to the danger it poses. With all major governments seized by domestic priorities, actions seriously capable of prevention or of crisis intervention have not been designed. Any attempt to do so would have signaled what is currently an unacceptable intent. As a result no one has prepared for what is apparently about to happen—the extension of fighting in Kosovo and Macedonia, its resurgence in Croatia, and the inevitable resonance in the surrounding region.

This situation is a looming crisis in international security arrangements for a series of fundamental reasons.

1. The root causes—the precipitous disintegration of authoritarian political systems and the induced transformation of once isolated economies—are new phenomena whose consequences are not fully understood.

154

2. With no agreed basis to assess either the magnitude of violence that could occur or the potential for constructive regeneration, the industrial democracies that would have to fashion an effective response have not been able to form the consensus judgment necessary to do so.

3. There is nonetheless a strong presumption that their interests are very powerfully engaged and that they will eventually be driven to uphold them. Industrial democracies cannot operate without defending standards of human rights and political procedure that are being egregiously violated. They cannot themselves prosper in an irreversibly internationalized economy if large contiguous populations descend into endemic violence and economic depression.

4. Because of these large underlying interests and predictable failure to prepare systematically, the United States and the Western European countries are particularly prone to crisis induced reactions chosen for their symbolic value and ease of execution rather than their decisive effect. Air Strikes and the arming of victims are plausible examples. If a dramatic episode produces a compelling impulse to act more assertively, the things that the Western democracies are in fact prepared to do, are much more likely to intensify and to propagate civil violence than to control it.

Predictable trouble of this sort creates special obligations for independent research institutions. It is our avowed purpose to anticipate emerging policy problems better than immediately responsible officials are likely to be able to do, to issue intelligible warning, and to induce relevant public discussion. I am not quite sure how urgently or extensively to respond to these obligations, but I do want to initiate a series of exploratory discussions.

As a focus for those discussions, let me outline two ingredients that an effective policy for controlling civil violence would have to have. These are, respectively, a justifying rationale and an appropriate operational design.

Justifying Principles

The problem presented is that of establishing basic civil order under circumstances where it has fundamentally broken down and is unlikely to be regenerated within reasonable time or at tolerable human cost. Intervention to accomplish such a purpose is necessarily a major intrusion. It runs the obvious risk of becoming the organizing focus of resistance and thereby self-defeating. If that is to be avoided, then the justifying purpose must be reliably persuasive. The difference between an intervention that succeeds and one that is destroyed by immune reaction would depend on the degree of spontaneous acceptance or rejection by the local population.

That point has two major implications. It means that any effective action would have to be broadly international in character. The risk of encountering decisive rejection is substantially greater for any single government or regional group than for the international community as a whole. It also means that the principles used and the specific objectives derived from them must be sustained across different political and cultural traditions. With nationalist sentiments surging in the areas of greatest concern, a successful intervention or preventive action must be based on standards that can transcend those sentiments. As experience over the past several decades should have taught us, no amount of political will or military firepower can compensate for the failure to establish legitimacy.

What rationale could conceivably carry this burden? The answer, if there is one, presumably involves human rights so fundamental that they are not derived from any particular political or economic ideology. Those would have to do with life itself in its personal dimensions—food, clothing, shelter, physical protection, basic health services and family integrity. The presumed list would not include such matters as freedom of speech and of political association which have been the more prominent preoccupation of Western governments.

This implies, then, a new standard for organizing international relationships. Any government that fails to provide the most fundamental rights for major segments of its population can be said to have forfeited sovereignty and the international community can be said to have a duty in those instances to reestablish it. If the absence of functional sovereignty is declared in any situation, assertive measures to recreate it would be allowed, measures that would not be allowed for narrower, less fundamental objectives.

There are, of course, a large number of practical problems with this formulation. How is the set of fundamental rights to be determined? The most relevant document—the Universal Declaration of Human Rights— is certainly authoritative in principle but nonetheless is too inclusive for the purpose in question. Some selection would have to be made from the rights it proclaims to justify assertive international intervention. Moreover, assuming the selection is accomplished, how would the absence of sovereignty be credibly declared? What specific criteria would regulate the declaration? How is Chinese behavior in Tibet or the Los Angeles riots or the presence of homeless people on the streets of most major cities to be prevented from triggering the mechanism? In addition there is no guarantee that practical solutions to these problems would confer the organizing power intended. There is ample evidence of murderous emotions being able to override any sense of fundamental rights. Indeed that is generally what happens when state structures break down.

Perhaps, then, the only claim that can reasonably be made at this point is that we cannot afford to dismiss the suggested standard summarily. Assuming that the problem will not be indefinitely ignored, some standard like this must eventually be developed.

Operational Design

The assertive protection or reconstitution of civil order would also extend the international community and its member states well beyond any experience to date with military operations. If the suggested standard were accurately and responsibly used, the functional absence of sovereignty would not only be a legal assertion but also a social fact. That means that traditional strategic operations to deter or intimidate or attack a coherently managed opponent could not be effective. They require an opposing political structure to work their intended effect. Established peacekeeping operations have the same requirement and fail for the same reason.

The violence in Bosnia and in Somalia is being conducted by irregular militia with command discipline too loose to be effectively controlled by any central leadership. Reflecting the breakdown of civil order these militia attack unarmed victims as much or more than similarly armed opponents. They would be no match for professional military units in a field engagement, but in Bosnia at least and in other areas of the former Yugoslav republic they could be a major threat if they chose to conduct guerilla operations.

Establishing civil order requires that these militia be disarmed and disbanded to some reasonable approximation. They at least would have to be deprived of armed vehicles and heavy weapons. Accomplishing that objective and maintaining standard civil law in support of relief operations would be the basic military mission of an intervention force. That would necessarily have to be accompanied by a process for reconstituting a valid government, presumably to be organized in parallel.

This mission would impose some unique but predictable requirements on an international force organized to conduct it. The operation would have two distinct phases—a very assertive operation to disarm the militia followed by a more reassuring one designed to preserve civil order.

The first phase, if it is to be successful, would have to be relatively short. Almost by definition a pacification campaign that does not succeed quickly will not succeed at all. An international force to conduct this phase would have to be able to initiate combat and would have to have sufficient personnel, firepower, mobility, and above all information resources to do so decisively. It would also have to have the command sophistication and operational discipline to do it judiciously. The point is not to track down and destroy every marauding band but rather to defeat a few in order to intimidate and cajole the rest. The operation needs to be designed both to induce fear among those inclined to resist and to convey reassurance to those inclined to accommodate. Neither message is easy to convey to dispersed, poorly integrated opponents and both require strong measures to be broadcast effectively. The balance between them is vital.

There is no close precedent for a military operation that has these properties, certainly not for one with the degree of international character required to meet requirements of legitimacy. Advanced national military establishments have the component skills and capacities required but have not designed operations of this sort and have not practiced them. Achieving the integral international cooperation necessary would add to the burdens of doing so but would also offer some benefit in breaking out of established operational doctrines. The obvious point is that the preparation required would take several months to complete and therefore imposes an unescapable burden of anticipation on political leaders.

The second phase of the operation, keeping basic order in the aftermath of a pacification campaign, is more routine and has more precedent. The problem is less that of designing it than of sustaining it. Since it would be difficult to impose any schedule on the parallel process of reconstituting a viable sovereign government, this phase could be an extended one, and participating parties would worry about an indefinite commitment. In this case the requirements of legitimacy are a clear advantage. A force designed to preserve an enforced peace could be composed of many national units on a rotating basis. Individual countries could be given a time limit for their commitment and burden-sharing arrangements could be introduced—initial commitments might be made shorter in duration than subsequent ones, for example, to reflect what would presumably be a greater risk in establishing the operation than in continuing it.

The military operations required by both phases can in principle be designed, but it is predictable that current national governments will be very reluctant to initiate the effort. No existing military organization will be eager for this assignment. It seems important, therefore, to induce some serious public discussion so that at least the basic requirements will be recognized.

John Steinbruner

Brookings Foreign Policy Studies
November 1992

Appendix D

Humanitarian Emergencies and Assistance

Hundreds of thousands, indeed millions of the civilian population in Africa fall victim to humanitarian tragedies, often resulting from civil wars, communal violence and other forms of social upheavals. As a result, these people are being deprived of the fundamental necessities of life, such as food, shelter, clothing, physical security, basic health care, and the integrity of the family. Some of this tragic suffering results from such natural calamities (drought, flood, earthquakes, and environmental hazards). But by far the most devastating and often unremedied causes are those that relate to political cleavages and confrontations in other words, human-made disasters.

The moral and legal obligation to provide emergency assistance to these innocent victims must in the first place rest with the governments of the countries concerned. In the cases of natural calamities, governments will normally act promptly to provide or mobilize the needed emergency relief, often in collaboration with international agencies. However, in cases of internal conflicts where the governments have either collapsed or are themselves partial and the affected population often identified with the adversary, domestic relief services may be unavailable or even actively resisted and a positive response to offers of international assistance cannot be guaranteed. Human rights may be further violated in consequence.

Today, media access and the burgeoning of NGO activities have created a situation where the pressure of international public opinion is increasingly prompting the international community to demand humanitarian action on both moral and political grounds.

The critical questions for the international community then become: what degree of humanitarian suffering under what conditions should justify what form of international action, by whom, through what operational mechanisms and with what precise objectives? This means clarifying the principles, the organizational framework, the operational doctrine, and the precise goals of such intervention.

The clarification of the principles would provide guidelines or standards on what would trigger and justify intervention. The organizational framework raises questions as to who would initiate the decision making process for intervention, and once approved, who would conduct the operations. The issue of operations itself raises questions on the military or civilian forces to be used and their preparedness or training for the task. The issue of objectives raises the question of whether the operations should stop at meeting the short-term emergency needs or extend to addressing the causes of the crisis in order to reconstitute a self-sustaining system of public or civil order.

How should one define the threshold of human suffering beyond which the international community cannot stand by and watch? The following points could constitute a framework of standards that might guide future action by governments and international organizations in cases of humanitarian emergencies:

First: the principles of sovereignty and non-intervention in the international affairs of states should be upheld and reaffirmed by the international community. In that connection, responsibility for addressing international humanitarian tragedies must first and foremost rest with governments.

Second: sovereignty is not absolute, but instead must be seen as entailing certain responsibilities and obligations over the territory and the population, the responsible control of which justifies sovereignty in international law.

Third: failure to meet such fundamental responsibilities and obligations with the consequential suffering of masses of innocent people creates a right and an obligation on the part of the international community to act toward providing the needed protection and assistance. To facilitate decision-making on this issue, it is necessary to define in relatively precise terms the standards to be observed or whose violation would trigger an international response. Such a standard-setting could in itself be an effective deterrent to violation.

Fourth: humanitarian intervention should ideally be genuinely collective and be undertaken by the United Nations or under its authority.

Fifth: while addressing an emergency situation must remain a paramount objective, the international community should strive to create conditions that would ensure the normalization and sustainability of a civil order that meets minimum standards in providing protection and assistance to the masses of the affected population.

Sixth: there is a need to design rules of intervention that would serve the dual purpose of initial military pacification and the civilian role of reconstituting a functioning civil society and a self-sustaining public order.

Seventh: a government that refrains from seeking or welcoming international humanitarian assistance could be perceived to have failed in meeting its responsibilities and obligations. These ought to be assumed and exercised by the international community. There should thus be no essential conflict between the traditional concept of sovereignty and the right or obligation of the international community to intervene and offer protection and assistance.

High-Level Group of the
InterAction Council

South Africa
January 1993

Appendix E

Statement by the Representative of the Secretary-General

Mr. Chairman, thank you for giving me the floor to address the Commission for a second time.

Today, as the Commission concludes its discussion of this item and prepares to take a decision on the recommendations of the study, I would like to end my contribution by highlighting a few points.

Let me begin by expressing my deep appreciation for the many kind comments that have been made on the study. I would like to emphasize once more that although I worked hard on the study and hold myself fully responsible for the contents, I could not have been able to prepare the document before you within the short time available to me, if I had not availed myself of the contributions of many individuals and organizations. I repeat this not only to acknowledge them, but also because I believe their contribution symbolized the amount of good will behind the Commission's work on behalf of the internally displaced.

With respect to the substance of the matter, the magnitude of the crisis of internal displacement cannot be over-emphasized. This is self evident in the sheer numbers of the internally displaced, estimated last year at 24 million, reported this year as having risen to 25 million, and almost certain to have already exceeded this estimate. When compared to the number of refugees estimated last year at 17 million, these are indeed staggering figures. But there is more to the crises than the figures indicate. During my on-site visits to several countries, I was reminded several times in different contexts that the international community should always remember that behind the statistics are human beings in desperate need of protection and assistance. I have seen these people in the most outrageous conditions of deprivation and indignity.

But perhaps the true magnitude of the crisis for the countries concerned can be better understood if it is realized that while the internally displaced are the worst hit, the most frequent causes of displacement—armed conflict, civil strife and communal violence—are afflictions from which the nation as a whole ultimately suffers. Human rights violations constitute a major cause, but more often than not, they are the result of other devastating causes. Natural causes also uproot people, but assistance and protection for the victims are more readily available. Consequences must be related to the causes, if the problems are to be tackled at the roots. Meanwhile, however, those who suffer the most must receive immediate attention. Treating symptoms is never the solution, but it cannot be postponed until the causes are eradicated.

This raises the issue of definition on which a number of delegations focused attention. While I share their concern with the need for a definition, this should not be a reason for delaying action by the Commission. The issue is whether one should first define and then look, or find and then define. Most certainly, the way out of the dilemma must be to act on both fronts simultaneously. This is why I favor a flexible working definition that provides indicators for identifying those needing protection and assistance, without adopting a conclusive or rigid definition. What is important is that needy people not be excluded. It is better to err on the side of inclusion than exclusion.

The question of whether or not existing international human rights and humanitarian law provides adequate protection is another debatable issue. As I pointed out in my earlier remarks, this debate is both descriptive and normative. Descriptively, opinion is divided between those who believe that there is enough coverage in existing law and those who see significant gaps. Normatively, some people believe that to admit the existence of gaps would be to provide loopholes, since governments cannot be held accountable for violation of non-existing law. Others are convinced that recognizing the inadequacy of existing law not only focuses attention on the problem of displacement, but also provides an opportunity for developing a targeted protection. Again, I believe that the way out of this dilemma is to build on both assumptions by first compiling the laws that now exist in scattered international instruments, analyzing them in relation to the specific needs of the internally displaced, and developing from them a more targeted statement of principles or code of conduct. This could then lead to the preparation of a declaration and ultimately a more legally binding instrument. The bottom line is that there is at present no legal instrument focused on the specific needs of internally displaced persons.

The issue of mechanism, though not without controversy, is less disputed. Everyone would agree that while important services are being rendered by a number of organizations and institutions, foremost among whom are UNHCR and ICRC, no entity is mandated to cater specifically for the needs of the internally displaced. This is clearly a major gap in the international system.

Ideally, the internally displaced merit the same degree of international attention as is now accorded refugees. But since such a major institutional arrangement does not seem likely in the foreseeable future, action by the Commission within the framework of its mechanisms is the most practical. And among the existing mechanisms, the one so far chosen by the Commission, that of a Representative of the Secretary-General, appears to be well suited as a focal point and a link with the pertinent bodies within the UN system.

In this context, it is my firm belief that the task of the Representative of the Secretary-General should involve keeping in touch with the realities on the ground through country visits, engaging in a dialogue with the governments and other pertinent actors, working in close cooperation with the relevant international organizations, and otherwise pursuing practical measures for improved protection and assistance of the internally displaced. It is true that it will not be easy to combine the monitoring and reporting role with that of dialogue, but a concerted effort that brings all these functions into cooperative focus is essential. One must assume that there is a minimum common ground of good will and humanitarian concern on which joint efforts to provide protection and assistance can be based. And indeed, as some have pointed out, protection and assistance go hand in hand in much the same way as human rights and humanitarian concerns are inseparable. This should alleviate the concern sometimes expressed over issues of national sovereignty.

Mr. Chairman, the masses of the internally displaced who suffer from severe deprivation, degradation and even physical insecurity are people without a voice in international circles. Their only voice is the collective conscience of humanity of which the Commission on Human Rights is a focal point. I have seen their yearning for help and how their hopes and aspirations were lifted by the sight of the UN representatives arriving by planes or vehicles with the United Nations flag or emblem. I witnessed this in my travels with Mr. Mazowiecki, the Special Rapporteur on the former Yugoslavia, and I saw it during my own visits to camps and villages in other countries. The message that they are no longer beyond the reach of the international community in general and the United Nations in particular has been delivered. The question now is how this message can be translated into practical results that would provide them with protection and assistance. Failure to do so can only cause more anxiety and despair than might have been the case before their hopes and aspirations were raised.

Let me end on an optimistic and challenging note, building on a personal experience. I began my professional career some twenty-six years ago in the United Nations Secretariat as a Human Rights Officer. Comparing the work of the Commission then and now, I can say without hesitation that humanity has come a long way. Those who endeavored to make this possible have a great deal to be proud of.

That is the optimistic side. The challenging side is that there is, needless to say, a great deal more to be done.

I hope I am not being presumptuous or too moralistic when I say that governments come and go, individuals move from one spectrum of representation to another, but certain fundamental causes remain on the high ground of humanity and humanitarianism. I say this as one who has represented my country as Ambassador to Canada, Scandinavian countries and the United States of America and as Minister of State for Foreign Affairs for a number of years. I have had the honor to speak for my country in many international gatherings.

Many years from now, as some of us will reflect back on the challenging decisions the Commission is called upon to make today, the question will arise as to whether or not governments and their representatives stood behind the efforts to improve protection and assistance for the tragic victims of internal displacement or tried to stop the wheels of progress from rolling. I have no doubt which side most of us would rather be.

I thank you.

Francis M. Deng

Geneva
March 1993

Index